At a time in history when humans are more affluent, healthier, and have never been more in command of nature, levels of depression, anxiety, and despair are higher in the West and developing world than they have ever been. *Practicing Resurrection* penetrates this irony with gospel hope. Writer, teacher, and spiritual guide Jeanie Miley ushers the reader through life's dramas, drawbacks, and devastations with an engaging and encouraging style of writing. The compelling narrative of her own experiences and insights into hope are illumined by lyrical reflections of God's faithfulness through the life, death, and resurrection of Jesus Christ. The fruit of a lifetime of faithful ministry through writing, *Practicing Resurrection* is another gift from Jeanie Miley of grace and hope.

—Brad Creed, President
Campbell University

Jeanie's book is a wonderful reminder that God can be found in the everyday experiences of life. Jeanie weaves emotions, wisdom, Scripture, and years of experience into stories that help the reader to see God with new eyes. It is through Jeanie's stories of laughter, challenging conversations, travel, movies, tragedies, the death of dear friends, or a walk in the outdoors that the reader catches glimpses of a God who is present, active, and full of life—drawing us ever toward hope and resurrection.

—Karen G. Massey, Associate Dean
McAfee School of Theology, Mercer University

Resurrection happens. Jeanie Miley leads us to explore the creative impulse of a loving God who, with tenderness and surprise, will bring us back to life over and over in the course of our imperfect life pilgrimages. This book helps the reader be on the lookout for signposts of resurrection and the creative future awaiting each pilgrim.

—Suzii Paynter, Executive Coordinator
Cooperative Baptist Fellowship

Smyth & Helwys Publishing, Inc.
6316 Peake Road
Macon, Georgia 31210-3960
1-800-747-3016
©2017 by Jeanie Miley
All rights reserved.

Library of Congress Cataloging-in-Publication Data

Names: Miley, Jeanie
Title: Practicing resurrection : radical hope in difficult times / by Jeanie
Miley.
Description: Macon : Smyth & Helwys, 2017.
Identifiers: LCCN 2017025203 | ISBN 9781573129725 (pbk. : alk. paper)
Subjects: LCSH: Resurrection. | Hope--Religious aspects--Christianity. |
Spiritual formation.
Classification: LCC BT873 .M55 2017 | DDC 234/.25--dc23
LC record available at https://lccn.loc.gov/2017025203

JEANIE MILEY

Practicing

RESURRECTION

[*Radical Hope in*
Difficult Times]

Also by Jeanie Miley

Dedicated with gratitude and love

to Frank Pool,

who embodied radical hope

and the power of resurrection . . .

who lived to the end

with a belief in *what's next*

and with uncommon faith and trust

in the love and power of a merciful and gracious God

Acknowledgments

*Now faith is confidence in what we hope for
and assurance about what we do not see.*
Hebrews 11:1

The body of Christ, the church in the world, has taken multiple hits through history and especially in the last thirty years. The church has been buffeted about by denominational conflicts, sea changes in society, the impact of television and technology, the unholy alliances of politics and religion, scandals within various religious institutions, the mega-church phenomenon, and the rise of fundamentalism.

With the clamor of voices declaring the decline in church attendance or affiliation and the rise of biblical illiteracy, I remain hopeful for the authentic church, and my hope is alive and well because I have been closely connected to the living and breathing communities of faith I grew up in. Hope has grown stronger in me because of my investment and participation in the various churches of my lifetime, imperfect as they might be.

The beliefs I describe in this book formed when I was a child growing up in the warmth and nurture of a local church. I have spent my entire life deeply connected to a community of faith, and for those in my history who informed and nurtured my spiritual formation, I am deeply grateful.

For you, the people of Southland Baptist Church in San Angelo, Texas, I give thanks. With you, we dared to create a new church, participating with each other and the Spirit of God in establishing a family of faith built on the love of God, love for each other, and freedom in Christ. With our faith firmly set in the belief that God had called us to the work, we set out with our various dreams and desires to birth and nurture a church that would be bigger than a building and sturdier than any institution. I treasure the memories of that privilege and the ways in which I learned with you what it means to hope for what you cannot yet see, and then watched that infant church grow into the sturdy church it is today.

For the people of River Oaks Baptist Church in Houston, Texas, I am so grateful. With you over these twenty-five years, I have learned that the real power is to be found in the depths of one's heart, and that the hope that matters is found by cultivating the presence of the Living Christ within. It has been with you that I have learned what really matters are not the numbers and appearances, but the intangible and immeasurable gifts of love and joy and peace. With you, I have shared so many joys and sorrows, celebrations of life and love, and the pain of tragedies and the deep griefs that accompany death. With you, I have experienced the wonders of the Mystery of Christ, who continues to extend without measure mercy, grace, and love. With you, I have learned that while we humans still look on the outside, God looks on the heart. You have allowed me the freedom to learn, grow, ask, seek, and knock, and it has been in that freedom that I have learned what it means to hope.

And to my parents, Helen and Louis Ball, I am so grateful to have been born to you and to learn from you what hope is all about. I absorbed more than your optimism. I witnessed your strong faith, and the quiet and clear evidence of your hope in Christ. Your unwavering trust in God and your willingness to surrender to the guidance of the Holy Spirit formed my faith. It was you who taught me first and taught me most about the power of hope and how to keep hope alive, all the way to the end of your lives. How can I keep from singing? I didn't know what you were teaching me at the time, or how profoundly you taught me by your actions, but I know it now. Maybe, in ways too mysterious for words, you know that I learned them. From you, I caught the ways of faith and hope.

To them God has chosen to make known among the Gentiles the
glorious riches of this mystery, which is Christ in you, the hope of glory.
Colossians 1:27

I am deeply grateful.

CONTENTS

PREFACE

Writers Juan Gabriel Vásquez and Rabih Alameddine held an audience spellbound at the Alley Theatre in Houston, Texas, on the night of November 21, 2016. Reading from their current bestsellers and then engaging in an interview and dialogue with a professor from the Creative Writing program of the University of Houston, both novelists spoke passionately about their work, their cultures, and the different roles writers play in different cultures.

Sponsored by Inprint, these writers joined a lineup of bestselling authors brought to Houston through the Margaret Root Brown Reading Series. Each was asked by the interviewer what he or she would say to a writer in America today.

While both of these writers gave practical wisdom, it was Vásquez whose words inform me as I offer this book about the practicing resurrection and keeping hope alive.

A native of Colombia, Vásquez spoke from the cultural and political world of Latin America, contrasting the role of novelist and writer in his world to that of a writer in America. His words inspire and instruct me daily.

"I will tell you this," Vásquez, his voice filled with passion. "If you feel an urgency about something, you must write about it!"

I have written this book with a keen sense of urgency about doing what I can with what I have, where I am, to keep hope alive.

The words of Thomas Merton also inspire me: "I stand among you as one who offers a small message of hope . . . ." Merton offered his message of hope through his life and his work, and my guess is that even he would be astounded at how many lives he inspired to share hope with others. I count myself among them, and so I pass along the hope others have inspired in me.

As I write, the prayer attributed to St. Francis of Assisi, words certainly consistent with his spirit and his work, informs me.

> Lord, make me an instrument of your peace.
> Where there is hatred, let me sow love.
> Where there is injury, pardon.
> Where there is doubt, faith.
> Where there is despair, hope.
> Where there is darkness, light.

It is my prayer that this book will stir and encourage hope and eyes to see evidence of hope.

INTRODUCTION

Practicing resurrection is a way of being in the world,
a mindset, a heartset, an attitude,
a way of choosing and behaving and speaking, and the way of radical
hope.

Practicing resurrection is about living as a person of hope
in the world, in everyday life
and even when everything argues against hope.

Practicing resurrection is evidence of being Easter people.
We who claim to be followers of Christ
are not life/death people.
We are life/death/Life people.
We who dare to call ourselves Christians must feel the urgency of the
moment.
We who presume to be carriers of his love must be instruments of hope.
We who have been saved, redeemed, healed, transformed, liberated, and
empowered
by the Living Christ
are under a holy imperative to live as if we really do believe what we
declare:
Through the mystery of the resurrection, he is alive in us, with us,
through us . . .
And so it is that our hope is in him.

Therefore, we are called to practice resurrection and help God keep
hope alive,
where we are, one day, one hour, one breath at a time.
It is my belief that God is counting on us for such a time as this.

Chapter 1

WHENEVER POSSIBLE . . . DANCE

On a muggy August night in 2015, my husband and I watched from our hotel balcony as a dramatic storm swept across Santa Fe, New Mexico, splitting the sky with flashes of lightning and loud, rumbling thunder. Fascinated by the beauty and mesmerized by the drama of the storm, we lingered on the balcony for the light show. Soon, however, falling temperatures and a driving rain chased us inside.

Both rested and energized by a vacation in Colorado, we had stopped in Santa Fe for a couple of nights on our way home. We got ready for bed, but the peacefulness of the night was interrupted by a phone call from a friend and member of our church in Houston.

It's never good news when the phone rings after 10 p.m., and on this night, the devastating news that our friend Terry Stewart had been in a plane crash split our hearts and turned the night into a long, terrible waiting via long distance with Terry's wife, Gail, and their two daughters, both of whom we had known since they were babies. We finally learned Terry did not survive.

Terry was an experienced pilot and a steady hand for any event, and on this day he was flying between Boulder and Steamboat Springs in pursuit of the certification necessary to fly into the mountains of

Colorado. The Piper PA-28 Cherokee plane he and his instructor were in crashed into a ravine called Rabbit Ears Pass.

The shock and devastation for family and friends were terrible, and the hundreds of us who gathered to support the family felt the loss of the good, faithful, funny, and kind man who was also creative, loyal, and life-loving. We tried to hold each other up while the harsh reality and the unbearable loss, sank into our minds and hearts. Our church family, shocked and traumatized, gathered to offer what comfort we could to each other and to Terry's family, but his death was hard on all of us.

Hope is not a feeling of certainty that everything ends well. Hope is just a feeling that life and work have meaning.

—Vaclav Havel

As we walked away from the cemetery, the hard work of grieving stretched out into an unwanted terrain, but all who love must eventually face this passage.

In other cultures, I am told, grieving people are allowed a year to mourn, and in a variety of ways. In American culture, we generally allow people a couple of weeks to "get over" the death of a loved one, and then we expect them to pull themselves together and get back to work. In our culture, people often push grief down into the depths of their hearts and out of their minds, but often into their bodies. We try to get through the long process of grieving "as best we can," as one grieving person told me.

There is a time to weep and a time to laugh, a time to mourn and a time to dance.

Ecclesiastes 3:17

Sometimes one's best doesn't feel good enough, but all of us, struck by grief, do what we can do.

Over the next year, day by day, Gail and the girls and Terry's mother walked that perilous pathway of mourning, and we who love them offered what we could. The light at the end of the first year was Kelsey's wedding to Aaron, an event that the whole family had been eagerly and joyfully anticipating.

As both the daughter of a minister and the wife of a minister, I often have the opportunity to be on the inside of the struggles of a minister before, during, and after funerals and weddings. On the occasion of this wedding so soon after Terry's death, a tender and vulnerable haze settled over the wedding planning and preparations.

"I must say something about Terry," my husband, Martus, said to me as he prepared the special words for this wedding. "His absence is on everyone's mind, but I don't want what I say to take away from the joy of the occasion or the celebration." He and I talked about what would be appropriate.

The church was packed on the night Kelsey and Aaron were married. Every detail of the wedding ceremony was perfect— the flowers, the music, the lovely bridesmaids and handsome groomsmen, Gail's dress, everything—and when Gail walked her firstborn down the aisle, a palpable sense of the moment and a holy hush came over the friends and family who were gathered to celebrate the happy occasion and to extend love and support to our beloved friends.

Weeping may remain for a night, but joy comes in the morning. . . . You turned my wailing into dancing; you removed my sackcloth and clothed me with joy.

Psalm 30:5b, 11

As Gail and the bride and groom met at the altar with Martus, I could hardly breathe. "Kelsey, I'm not your dad," my husband began, "but I am a dad and Terry was my friend, and I can say to you with full assurance tonight that if he were here he would tell you how beautiful you are and how much he loves you and wants you and Aaron to be happy."

"There wasn't a dry eye in that place," a friend said afterward, and I'm pretty sure he was right. I couldn't have seen any others' tears because my eyes were flooded with my own.

After the vows were exchanged and Kelsey and Aaron were declared to be husband and wife, we moved from the church to the reception. The weather was perfect, the mood was festive, and meal was fabulous. The decorations were beautiful, and the celebration was jubilant.

When it was time for the dancing to begin, we joyfully applauded the bride and groom.

And then it was time for the father-daughter dance.

The gaiety quieted, and, almost in one movement, the crowd moved to circle the wooden dance floor as Kelsey and her mom solemnly walked to the center.

I held my breath. We waited for the music. No one moved.

What were they—mother and daughter—going to do?

The band began to play at a slow tempo and then picked it up a bit when Kelsey and her mom walked toward each other.

The groomsmen encircled the dance floor as Gail and Kelsey moved to the beat of the music, separately and gracefully. I exhaled slightly.

Suddenly and surprisingly, the band picked up the tempo to "Shop Around" and Kelsey moved to the jaunty beat, dancing over to one of the groomsmen as if to choose him. However, Gail danced quickly and smoothly to her daughter, pulling Kelsey away and shaking her head and her hand to the beat of "My mama told me . . . 'You better shop around!'"

> *If we are willing, the experience of grief can deepen and widen our ability to participate in life.*
>
> —John Claypool

The crowd burst into laughter and applause, but the dance wasn't over.

From one groomsmen to the next, Kelsey danced, only to be pulled away by her mom just as the singer belted out, "My mama told me, 'You better shop around!'" until finally, the bride danced over to her groom, and with that, Gail raised her arms in approval and the crowd roared with laughter and joy.

In that moment, it was as if Gail announced to all of us, "The time of mourning is past; it is time to celebrate!" And did we ever celebrate.

Was the loss of Terry any less biting with that celebration? Absolutely not! However, Terry would have wanted the marriage of his daughter to be celebrated to the hilt.

Will the Stewarts ever stop missing Terry? Never.

Forever, that terrible event will be a marker in the lifelines of all of us who knew Terry and loved him, and we will say such things as "Remember when Terry took those Pampers and cases of formula to the food pantry?" and "Remember how much Terry loved a party?" We will remember too how much he loved fine food and good wine, Paris and Nice, and all things French.

Times like this test faith and test it hard. Some people become more tender, more open, more compassionate and experience a deepening faith in God. Other people turn to substances to numb the pain or to distractions to keep them from having to face the losses they think they cannot bear. Some get stuck in the grief, as if in concrete, unable to move through the anger, depression, fear, and sorrow to accept the one thing they never wanted to face.

> *To hope means to be ready at every moment for that which is not yet born, and not become desperate if there is no birth in our lifetime.*
>
> —Erich Fromm,
> *The Revolution of Hope: Toward a Humanized Technology*

I watched Gail and her family walk through the dark valley of the reality of death. I know them as people of faith, and I watched their support of each other grow through the process of getting used to a world without Terry. They have taught me a lot about what I am calling the "resurrection principle" and what poet Wendell Berry means when he counsels us to "practice resurrection" in his poem "Manifesto: The Mad Farmer Liberation Front."

Terry taught us all about celebrating life, enjoying friendship, and doing acts of mercy and kindness for each other. He was a man who had his priorities straight, and he knew how to put first things first. He was also a man of faith, and it was a practical faith that he lived out by doing for others. I didn't realize it at the time because we were all so busy, but in looking back, I see that Terry taught me a lot in the years that I knew him.

The ones closest to him—the family he treasured—have taught me about this resurrection principle as they have learned more than they ever wanted to know about living through the shock and horror of Terry's sudden death. They have walked through these months and years of learning to live with the terrible, sometimes unbearable loss.

This family has been on my mind as I have written every chapter of this book.

They have been living proof of the power of *practicing resurrection.*

Questions to Ponder

1. When was the last time an event jarred you out of your comfort zone and propelled you into uncharted terrain?

2. Have you ever lost hope? How would you describe that feeling?

3. When someone you know experiences a life-altering event, in what ways do you provide comfort, presence, and understanding?

4. When a tragedy occurs, do you look for the reason it happened or try to understand what the event means for you and for others involved?

5. In what ways have you experienced the presence or action of God in the midst of trauma or heartbreak?

Up against the wall I am
Feeling trapped and stuck and barely remembering
life before that terrible moment . . .
        and knowing that from this day forward
        I will never not know what it was like
        not to feel the impact of this pain.
            God of mercy, God of grace!
            What can I do?
            Where can I go?
How can I move forward
when I can't escape this thing—
        this reality, this event,
        this loss, this situation?
I turn to the right and it turns with me.
I numb myself to sleep
and it's there when I wake
I turn to someone to ask a
            question . . .
and wonder if I will ever hear
anything that makes sense to me
again.
            God of mercy, God of grace!
All I can do is breathe! Does that count as prayer?

Chapter 2

I JUST KEPT SAYING YES

It was opening night in Chartres, France.

Still in awe that I was making my third pilgrimage to Chartres to walk the ancient labyrinth and participate in a Veriditas-sponsored workshop led by Phil Cousineau and Lauren Artress, I sat in a circle of new friends and fellow pilgrims in one of the meeting rooms of our hotel, the old stone monastery Maison St. Yves.

I was so pleased that MJ McGregor was going to facilitate my small group. Two years before, MJ had led our group that met in her apartment, which was a short walk from the cathedral. I knew something about her study and experience regarding the labyrinth and Chartres Cathedral and had loved her gentle, wise leadership of the previous group.

"How did you get here?" my friend Helen Fraser asked the leader of the small group as we pulled our chairs into a circle.

I waited to see where MJ would begin, eager to hear her account. I expected her to tell us a lot about her history and her rich experience and study, but she surprised me with her answer.

Hesitating for only a few seconds, MJ said, "I just kept saying yes!"

And my heart skipped a beat.

❁ ❁ ❁

I have a history with *yes*. Granted, I have a history with *no* as well, and *no*, rightly said, is important, but it is my history with *yes* that matters most to me.

I was challenged early in my young adulthood by the words of the former secretary of the United Nations Dag Hammarskjold when he said he had only two prayers, *Thank you* and *Yes*.

I have been guided by the wisdom of a friend who told me that you have to be willing to say *no* to something you may want and even something you think you may not be able to live without in order to say a Holy *yes*. I learned from Oswald Chambers that you have to say *no* to the good and even the better in order to say *yes* to the best.

When my first grandchild, Abby, was a toddler, just learning to run and talk, she taught me something about *yes*. When offered a trip to the park, an ice cream cone, a new book, or time in a swing, Abby would run toward that thing repeating, "Yes! Yes!" Her joyful response taught me an aspect of what Jesus meant when he said that being childlike—open, spontaneous, welcoming—was key to entering the kingdom of God.

Growing up in my religious tradition, I heard an emphasis on inviting Christ into our hearts. "He is always inviting us," my father said during the invitation at the end of a sermon. "Say yes to him."

Only weeks before I heard MJ's response to my friend's question, my spiritual teacher Keith Hosey responded to my account of a particular struggle with this simple wisdom: "Jeanie, say yes sooner!"

The way MJ answered the question caught my attention. Her response was so natural, just like Abby's response when I offered her something that made her happy.

Clearly, MJ's ability to lead discussions about the cathedral and facilitate our small group for a week didn't happen with one *yes*! It was not a one-time assent to one invitation that had shaped her pilgrimage; what mattered was that she *kept* saying yes. It was the continuous response, one *yes* at a time, that had brought her to that moment in Chartres.

My guess is that while her response was easy in that moment, there were also questions and even struggles getting to *yes*. Maybe she had also had to say *no* at times.

MJ's response shaped my mind and heart and direction for my pilgrimage that week and into the next week as well.

You just never know when a few words can be the very words a person needs to hear.

Only a few days later, I sat with my small group again, talking about grand things such as meaning and purpose and the ways in which walking the labyrinth had parallels with walking the pilgrimage of life. In the days between our first conversations with each other and this day, we had listened to deep wisdom from both Phil Cousineau, author of the classic *The Art of Pilgrimage*, and Lauren Artress, founder and creative director of Veriditas and author of *Walking a Sacred Path: Rediscovering the Labyrinth as a Spiritual Tool*, and so our conversations naturally turned to serious topics.

As in many of the conversations I had during 2016, the conversations soon turned to scary topics such as ISIS and Brexit, the presidential campaign in the United States, the breakdown of the systems we had all looked to for stability and security. Coming from different parts of the world and certainly different religious experiences and cultures, we found

Always be prepared to give a reason for the hope that is in you.

1 Peter 3:15b

common ground as we tried to integrate the inspiring and hopeful material we had heard with the serious state of the world. Soon, our tones grew anxious, and the conversation was filled with worry, stress, and almost dread.

Outside, the day was cold and dreary and the rain peppered the windows of the classroom.

In my small group, we grew more pensive and troubled as we talked, rendered quiet in the face of so many big things over which we knew we had no control. Inevitably, someone brought up the issue of "the kind of world in which our children and grandchildren will grow up," and the mood grew heavier.

"What can we do?" someone asked, and suddenly, the plaintive tone in her voice sparked something in me. I had to speak up, but I felt nervous about what I wanted to say.

Wrestling with the feelings of wanting to speak but being scared to speak, I finally said yes to the impulse that wouldn't go away. I recall now how forcefully I spoke, and it was with the same urgency with which I write this book.

"We who are the elders must show the way for the young ones. We who have hope must teach the children the practices of hope. Fear and despair will weaken all of us! We have a responsibility to live with faith and speak faith!"

Frankly, I surprised myself, both with the fervor that emerged from some place deep within me and also because I had not spoken up much in our group. Sometimes I am struck by shyness that lingers from childhood, holding me in its grip when I least expect it.

I confess here a bias: too much pessimism, too much negative talk, too much hopelessness repeated over and over get to me. It makes me break out in unpleasant feelings, unholy thoughts, strange anxieties, as if I am allergic to it.

Too much fear-talk, hate-talk, bashing, and trash-talk bother me. Such words suck energy out of a room and stir up nervousness in others. Too much bad-mouthing affects groups like verbal abuse affects us. The problems and patterns of domestic abuse, the cycle of violence in a family or a marriage, spill out into the culture, infecting with fear both innocent children and adults.

It's not that I'm a Pollyanna and unable to look square into the face of suffering. I am realistic optimist, and I believe that hope flourishes when I can call a spade a spade. I don't believe that avoidance of hard issues solves them. I know that sometimes we have to say hard things, and when the prevailing conversations are negative, hope dies.

My fervor was born in the conviction that I know words and attitude matter as we live our lives and face our challenges. My passion about helping the young build faith, hope, and trust comes from the conviction that it's important to our physical, mental, and emotional health to keep hope alive. It is often hope in the darkest, most difficult times that keeps a person alive.

I believe that Jesus knew what he was talking about when he said, "As a person thinks in his heart, so is he." I know that thoughts create actions, actions create habits, habits form character and shape a life, a day, a future.

I know that life is a constant challenge, and I know that learning how to say yes and keeping on saying yes is one of the ways to keep hope alive.

Knowing when to say yes and to what makes the difference.

Knowing to whom one says yes *matters most.*

When our entire pilgrimage group walked the labyrinth in the great cathedral in Chartres the next night, I pondered the mystery of being there, far from Houston, again. It had been thirteen years after the first time I heard of the Veriditas-sponsored labyrinth pilgrimages before I finally got to Chartres in 2011, and that time had been the fulfillment of a dream. I never imagined that I would be back again, much less two more times!

"Haven't you done that?" someone asked me before I left for this particular pilgrimage, and old messages from the past surfaced, messages that produced embarrassment that I was "getting to go to Chartres."

"Why do you want to do that again?" another person asked, and someone even said, "Wasn't once enough?"

"Why are you going this time?" a friend asked, and I tried to explain that I didn't know what I would receive this time. I knew it would be different from the other two times I had made that journey from Houston, Texas, to Chartres, France. "Can't you walk the labyrinths here in Houston?" the friend persisted.

And, in truth, I could. I have. The labyrinth as a pattern is fundamentally the same in every place. However, it is hard to explain what graces come when one is on pilgrimage. For me, the cathedral in

Chartres, and its labyrinth specifically, opens me to insights and truth in ways I haven't experienced anywhere else. I am incredibly blessed—incredibly privileged—to have been able to travel to France not once but three times for the sake of spiritual journey. My friends' confusion is understandable considering, at its core, I'm walking the same physical pattern I've walked before, and one I could walk without ever leaving Houston. And I know God would and does bless labyrinth pilgrimages here. If I were unable to travel beyond my city—as so many cannot because of health, finances, work, family, and countless other reasons—God would still bless my Houston labyrinth journey. But because I can return to Chartres, and remembering what God has done in my life there, I cherish the blessing of being able to return. The truth is that we never can predict what we might receive if we say yes to a journey. Not knowing is part of the leap of faith that makes pilgrimage exciting.

So it was that MJ's response in our small group—her *yes*—became my response. I had kept saying yes, and I have found that spiritual practice, whatever it is and whatever form it takes, is a way of saying yes to the Mystery, yes to life, and, as a result, yes to hope.

On this pilgrimage and on that particular night and in that sacred place with those specific fellow pilgrims, my prayer as I walked into the heart of the labyrinth was that I could release fears that might be blocking my living as a witness to hope and faith and trust, not only for my children and grandchildren but also for my own benefit.

I stood for a longer time than usual in the center of the labyrinth. I took in the candlelight that illuminated the cathedral I had come to love, and I memorized the play of light and shadows on the pillars and up into the high arches.

> *Hope's home is at the innermost point in us, and in all things. It is the quality of aliveness. It does not come at the end, as the feeling that results from a happy outcome. Rather, it is at the beginning as a pulse of truth that sends us forth.*
>
> — Cynthia Bourgeault,
> *Mystical Hope*

I breathed in the sounds of the musicians' voices and instruments, hoping to carry the beauty of the sensory experience home with me.

Standing in the center of the labyrinth, I opened my mind and heart to the mysterious presence of God. As a professed Christian, I attempt to follow the teachings of Jesus, and that qualifies me to count myself as an Easter person.

I am not, therefore, a life and death person. Being an Easter person means that I believe in life-death-Life! I believe in redemption. I believe in new beginnings, and I believe in transformation. I believe in not only the resurrection at the center of my religious faith but also that the historical event has implications for my life now.

My Christian worldview—how I see and understand and experience the world—is a point of view that is hopeful, life-giving, and expansive. It is based on one of my favorite Scriptures, which declares that "God is at work in all things, attempting to bring about good" (Rom 8:28).

Let me be clear: I have moments of disappointment, and I know what it is like to despair. I have known my own dark night of the soul; I know what it is like to feel abandoned, and I am far too familiar with what I felt was the silence and absence of God. I have experienced moments of depression, and as I write this I am deeply respectful of those for whom depression is a constant reality.

I know what it is like to cry out, "My God, my God, why have you forsaken me?" in the middle of the night, and I know what it is like to walk closely with people for whom the Presence of God is an almost impossible idea. I am acquainted with sorrow and struggle, grief and loss, and perhaps all of that is what makes me know the importance of *keeping on saying yes.*

The life of Jesus as recorded in the Gospels includes his birth and his life, his teachings, his death, his burial and resurrection. Jesus' life is central to my faith, and the reality of his Spirit dwelling within me and within all of creation is a firm tenet of my belief system. My worldview is based on the understanding that the mysterious presence and action of God that I call "the resurrection principle" is what enlivened Jesus after his death and can be seen in the entire Bible, from Genesis to Revelation.

The presence of God animates all of creation. It is the life force that thrums in every human being. It is the energy of love and grace and mercy. It is in the growth principle that informs a yearling that it is time to stand up and walk, and it is in the mind or the heart or the will of a grieving person who declares in one moment that he cannot go on and in the next finds it within himself to go on.

I can imagine that most anyone understands the concept of keeping hope alive, but I am using another term that adds a deeper spiritual reality to this idea: *practicing resurrection*. The idea of the "resurrection principle" came to me as I explored this belief in a yearlong study of God's actions in both the Old and New Testaments for the Thursday Morning Bible Study that I have now facilitated for twenty-five years.

When teaching a Bible study, I try to form a foundation from the Bible itself, and so I offer this one: The resurrection principle is the breath of God that bestowed life in the first humans and that is also found in the declaration and definition of God in Revelation 21:3: "Behold! I am making all things new."

The resurrection principle maintains that God is alive and active in all of creation. It is God in the midst of trouble and trauma, working for good.

The resurrection principle is the spiritual energy we call *hope*, placed there by God. It is the presence of God within us as Source and Life, providing us the resources to live the abundant life Jesus came to give us, to bear our sufferings, to work with the energies of God to bring about good. When it is time to walk confidently into our necessary and inevitable transitions in life—even the one at the end of life on this earthly plane, we trust steadily in the goodness and mercy of God.

When Paul the Apostle wrote in 1 Corinthians 13, "And now abide faith, hope and love," I believe he was acknowledging all three as gifts, graces, blessings of the Spirit of God, and I believe that those gifts are in us, in what Jesus called "the kingdom within."

What I carried to Chartres in early summer 2016 was a weary body and a mild case of burnout. Frankly, I was in a season of questions and concerns about the future, some doubts and leftover worries from the crises and challenges in the previous months.

I could have used a few days sitting by the ocean, simply watching the tide come and go, but I knew I needed to take my place on an airplane for a long-scheduled trip across the ocean and show up at a well-planned workshop with world-class leaders even when I wasn't fresh and full of vim, vigor, and vitality.

My pattern is that showing up for spiritual practice day after day, whether you feel God's presence or not, makes a difference; a long obedience in the same direction forms faith, enlivens hope, and empowers even a weak voice to say yes and to say it again.

My experience is that when I respond to the initiative of God to continue to keep on asking, keep on seeking, and keep on knocking, opening my mind and heart with the consent for God's presence and action in my life, I keep hope alive as well as the greatest power that exists in the universe—the power of love.

It's no wonder that my heart skipped a beat when MJ responded to my friend's question.

Her response sparked my imagination and warmed my heart.

Suddenly, I knew why I was there and I felt the energy of life and love—the presence of God—restoring my soul. I felt hope stirring in my heart once again.

I was there to say *yes* to life and to my life in a new way.

I was there to say *yes* to new experiences and to hope.

My *yes* on that labyrinth was my consent to have my mind and heart changed.

With the last vestiges of sunlight streaming through the stained glass windows and the candlelight illuminating the labyrinth, I turned again toward the Light, as a plant turns toward the sun.

Reflections

1. To what nudging do you need to answer with a firm *yes?*

2. What would happen if you decided to say a conscious and intentional *yes* to something every day?

3. In order to say *yes* to something you say you want, to what will you have to say *no?*

4. Where are you hesitating to do what you want to do and what you need to do? Consider the following passage: "Until one is committed, there is hesitancy, the chance to draw back, always ineffectiveness. Concerning all acts of initiative and creation, there is one elementary truth the ignorance of which kills countless ideas and splendid plans: that the moment one definitely commits oneself, then providence moves too. All sorts of things occur to help one that would never otherwise have occurred. A whole stream of events issues from the decision, raising in one's favor all manner of unforeseen incidents, meetings and material assistance which no man could have dreamed would have come his way. Whatever you can do or dream you can, begin it. Boldness has genius, power and magic in it. Begin it now." (Commonly attributed to Goethe, these sentences are more likely from W. H. Murray; see www.goethesociety.org/pages/quotescom.html.)

God-who-does-all-things-well,
    move me out of this inertia,
this frozenness,
this locked-up cell of fear or worry
or insecurity or grief or whatever
into which
I have voluntarily walked.
    I ask you to do for me what
    I cannot do for myself,
but then you remind me
that even you need my consent
my willingness
my surrender, my yielded self . . .
    Forgive me for expecting
    you to do for me what I am
    not willing to do.
Forgive me for holding back
playing games playing safe . . .
and even working against you.
    I'm moving forward, God.
    I'm saying Yes!
My prayer is Yes.
Lord, hear my prayer.

Chapter 3

PRACTICING RESURRECTION

On a warm June afternoon while touring the third-oldest Jewish synagogue in the United States, Congregation Miskve Israel in Savannah, Georgia, I purchased in the gift shop a brass paperweight shaped like the Hebrew word and symbol that means "life," Chai.

Carrying that symbol through the hallway of the synagogue, I could almost hear the music of *Fiddler on the Roof* and the voice of Tevye singing, "To life, To life!"

Indeed, life has a way of confusing us, blessing us, and bruising us, just as it has those who lived before us and as it will those who will come after us, and yet there is that fire in us, the life force itself, that wants to reach forward and even to toast and celebrate *life*.

Years later, that symbol still sits in a prominent place in our home. Following my visit to the synagogue, I called back to the gift shop and ordered more to give as gifts to friends who would appreciate the meaning of the symbol. I kept a stash of those symbols, often giving the gift in gratitude for some important way a friend had enriched my life or encouraged me when I was down,

> *I have come that you might have life . . . and have it to the full.*
>
> John 10:10

and at other times giving the gift as a sign and symbol of hope for someone who had lost her way or lost a loved one.

Always, that symbol has brought a light to the person's eyes.

While I write from a rich history within the Christian tradition, I am deeply conscious that the founder of my faith was a Jewish rabbi, so I am grateful to be part of a Judeo-Christian tradition. Judaism emphasizes the importance of enjoying life while on Earth. The common Jewish toast is *"l'chaim!"* which means *"To life!"* and it is said at celebrations in anticipation of good things to come.

On a street corner between my house and our church is a large modern house. In the yard of that house, prominently displayed, is a three-foot art piece in the shape of the Hebrew Chai. I have driven by that symbol for life countless times, and it always makes me smile.

Perhaps I will send the owners of that house a note, thanking them for placing the symbol in their yard.

For most of my life, the story of Lazarus, whom Jesus raised from death, had little meaning for me except as a Bible story that happened a long time ago. The story was interesting, but it had stayed flat on the pages of my Bible, stuck back in history as an important event in the lives of Mary, Martha, and their brother Lazarus, and for Jesus, but it didn't have anything to do with my life.

However, during a retreat at Laity Lodge in the Hill Country of Texas, I was leading a group in a guided meditation from my book *Becoming Fire.* As I stood in front of the adults who filled the Great Hall, I was planning to use another one of the stories in the Gospels as a setup for an afternoon of quiet and reflection. As I had done in other sessions, I was going to ask the retreatants to imagine themselves as the various individuals in the story, leading up to imagining what it would have been like to be with Jesus at that particular event.

When it's over, I want to say: all my life I was a bride married to amazement, I was a bridegroom, taking the world into my arms.

—Mary Oliver, "When Death Comes"

Much to my surprise, the Lazarus story suddenly came to my mind, and I began talking about what it must have felt to have been his sisters Mary and Martha, grief-stricken over the death of their brother and perhaps frustrated that Jesus had not come to them as quickly as they had wanted him to.

As I continued, the ancient story suddenly was lifted off the pages of the Bible. I imagined what it was like for Lazarus to have been in that tomb, hearing Jesus' voice calling his name. Suddenly, through the ways of mystery, that story became alive for me; suddenly, it had meaning for my life in the present tense!

What did Lazarus think and feel when he felt the life force take over in his body? What was it like for him to emerge from the darkness of the tomb into the light of day? What was it like for his neighbors and friends to free him from the death's wrappings, and what was that like for him?

In the years since that first experience of telling the Lazarus story, inviting the retreatants to go into the story with their imaginations and bring it to life in their own lives, I have come to see that at a deeply personal level, Lazarus in the tomb can be seen as the True Self in each of us that is buried within, wrapped in cultural expectations, family obligations, rigid roles, masks, defense mechanisms, labels we have worn, perhaps even curses we have picked up, been given, or even earned throughout a lifetime. Maybe someone whose approval we desperately wanted not only refused to give it but also kept up a lifetime of disapproval, almost as if casting a spell of low self-esteem or self-loathing.

What, I asked the retreatants on that warm summer day, does that story have to do with us if it can't come alive in us?

At the end of my words, the retreatants were to spend the afternoon in silence, walking the grounds, rowing or swimming in the river, praying, lounging in one of the hammocks, journaling, reading, or taking what the staff called power naps.

One by one, the retreatants slipped away, but one man stayed in his seat. I realized he was weeping, so I quietly sat beside him, waiting to see if he wanted to talk.

"I've spent my entire life hiding that I'm smart and wealthy," he said. "My life has been filled with tragedy, much of it public, and I've had to learn how to bear the pain of the family secrets becoming public." This man had an abundance of blessings, but those things made others jealous—yet had also given him incredible opportunities. He had endured public tragedies. There is irony that he felt he needed to hide the exceptional aspects of his life or even feel guilt—but his tragedies were exposed for the world to see.

He paused for a long time. I knew it was a holy moment.

"I wonder what would happen if I didn't have to hide who I really am," he mused, and I realized that my listening was a way of unwrapping a lifetime of death clothes that he had wound around his True Self.

"People always made fun of me because of the things I couldn't help—things I was born with!—and so I learned to hide who I am early," he said, and he wept.

It isn't just the things for which we feel shame or guilt, inferiority or inadequacy that we hide, but it is sometimes what Carl Jung called "the golden shadow," the gifts or unusual abilities, the particular opportunities or privileges we have been given that we learn to hide, sometimes even from ourselves.

Lazarus is a symbol of God's resurrection principle, working to bring the True Self within us to life, working to bring about what we have buried while working to achieve, accomplish, and acquire in the outer world what we have been told we should want and do.

Just as Jesus called forth the life of Lazarus from the tomb, so the mystery of God is available to each of us to empower and liberate us to live from the inside out. The mystery of God allows us to drop our masks, the false self, the image and persona we carry so we can live the life we were intended to live.

What makes a baby decide to stand up and walk one day?

What makes people want to thrive?

What made my friend Frank Pool, at age 98, ask me, "What are you going to do now?" or "What's next?"

I can easily explain how babies are designed to know when to sit up, crawl, walk, and then run. We are made with those impulses within us, impulses that direct us down the path of life.

We have within us the impulse to seek new adventures, to survive and thrive, to grow.

The life force in Frank Pool was so strong and so optimistic that even at his great age, his focus was on the future, what was to come, what new horizons needed to be seen or discovered.

We are born, I believe, with the resurrection principle within us. It is like a GPS guiding us forward, moving us along, helping us develop and grow and become the True Self we are meant to be.

❦ ❦ ❦

On a perfect Colorado summer afternoon in Lake City, my husband and I walked from the cabin where we were staying to the cabin of Dwain and Sybil Dodson for a conversation we didn't want to have.

On the way, memories from over thirty summers in Lake City rolled over and over in my mind. It was Frank Pool who had first introduced us to the tiny town nestled in the San Juan mountains in Colorado, and it was Dwain Dodson, our beloved pediatrician, who urged us to return summer after summer for rest and renewal. With both families, we share years of memories of jeep rides, moun-

And now these remain: faith, hope and love . . .

1 Corinthians 13:13

tain hikes, picnics, and fishing trips, and to each of them we are deeply grateful for the gifts of hospitality and memories.

As we approached the Cozy Cabin, I didn't want to go in. I didn't want to talk about what I knew Sybil and Dwain wanted to discuss, but love for these longtime friends made it both necessary and possible to have the dreaded conversation with our elderly friend whose health was failing.

Sybil and Dwain asked if Martus would do Dwain's funeral, and Dwain asked me to do his eulogy. Of course, we would have done anything for this friend who had given so much life and love and laughter to us, to our girls, and to hundreds of others throughout a lifetime.

When we left that day and walked back along Henson Creek to the cabin where we were staying with our children and grandchildren, I wept.

I believe in the power of the resurrection principle, but I also grieve hard when I have to let go of a beloved friend.

When we finally got the news of Dwain's death, Martus and I had to prepare for his service. I sat down with years of memories flooding my mind and with notes we had made since that day in Lake City. We knew that Dwain wanted the service to be uplifting and hopeful, and we knew that he wanted it built around the Scripture, "I am the resurrection and the life."

The marvelous richness of human experience would lose something of rewarding joy if there were no limitations to overcome. The hilltop hour would not be half so wonderful if there were no dark valleys to traverse.

—Helen Keller

Martus and I talked about what we would each say. For a man like Dwain, there was enough material for a dozen eulogies and a lengthy service.

"I'm going to center my thoughts on the resurrection principle that I observed in Dwain's love of nature, his resilience, and his medical practice," I said, and then was puzzled at the blank stare coming back at me.

"What do you mean?" Martus asked me. I was shocked.

I had taught a yearlong Bible study on Thursday mornings about this subject, but I realized in that moment that perhaps I had not fully communicated my ideas about the topic to him!

Martus knows I read a lot. He knows I like to research and learn from people beyond my training and religious tradition. I explained my idea of the resurrection principle only to have him ask, "Where did you get the idea of a resurrection principle? I've never heard it."

My friend and one-time publisher, Mark McElroy, introduced writer Wendell Berry to me. From that time until this, I have looked to Berry to challenge my narrow ideas and deepen my awareness through his novels, his essays, and his poetry.

Berry grew up on a Kentucky farm that had been in his family for five generations, and he now lives on a farm where he and his wife raised their children. As a university professor, cultural critic, and activist, Berry brings a broad view of life to his work, and I appreciate his prophetic boldness. Both his protests against what he sees as damaging to the human soul and the world as well as his affirmations for what he sees as life-giving and important make me want to live an authentic life firmly planted in my spiritual values.

Who knows what cultural crisis or religious chaos was going on around me when I first read Berry's poem, "Manifesto: The Mad Farmer Liberation Front," but I do remember how every line drew me in deeper. It was the last line that made me draw in my breath, however: "Practice resurrection."

This poem became guiding wisdom from then on, moving me out of getting stuck in any life problem and the worry that accompanied it to a position of hope.

I felt myself being swept up in hope because Berry's words were about actual actions I could take, things I could do when the rapids of change were sweeping away many systems, institutions, and families that I had looked to for love, security, and meaning.

Berry's poem was filled with jarring injunctions to live by if we don't want to make waves when everything around us is being taken over by someone who has values and intentions that don't match ours.

He tells us how to go along and get along with what is happening if we want to fit in, but we know that if we do those things and succumb to the creeping powers of an oppressive system, we die little by little.

After the first verse, Berry turns a corner and hands out instructions that come from a different place, a place of life and hope and possibility. They are instructions I could follow without losing the connection to my soul:

> So, friends, everyday do something that won't compute.
> Love the Lord. Love the world. Work for nothing . . .
> Love someone who does not deserve it . . .
> Give your approval to all you cannot understand . . .
> Ask the questions that have no answers.

Reading those words, I am called back to the life I want to live, to the values I want to manifest in my work, and to the attitude and spirit I want to animate my attitudes and emotions. From the first time I read the words of this poem, I knew that this poet knew what it was to lose a way of life. This man understood the shaking of the foundations of everyday life! And there was more.

> Invest in the millennium. Plant sequoias . . .
> Laugh . . .
> Be joyful though you have considered all the facts . . .
> Be like the fox who makes more tracks than necessary,
> some in the wrong direction.

I breathe more deeply when I read these words. I smile. I love every word of this poem and the rebel heart of the poet who refuses to be vanquished.

But that last line still stuns me and keeps taking my breath away. It challenges me to go beyond praying that God will give me faith and hope as nouns I can possess or feelings that will make me feel better. Berry's last directive is nothing less than a call to action, a "get-up-off-the-couch-and-move" wisdom saying captured in two words:

Practice resurrection.

It was when I first came to the last line of this poem that I gasped
and then sat in stunned silence in the penetrating holiness of the
moment. *This phrase was going to change my life.*

So it was that I set out on a journey of exploration and discovery
of just what it mean to *practice resurrection.*

"Jeanie, I've never heard anything about that—either in my theology
courses or any other of my seminary courses," he told me, as our
conversation about this new (to him) idea of "practicing resurrection" continued. I responded, "Well, now you have."

To be clear, I have already defined the ways I have experienced
God-at-work in the lives of human beings, but to expand the idea
of this "resurrection principle," it is helpful to identify the ways that
principle affects human beings.

I gave a simple definition of what I call the resurrection principle
in an earlier chapter. Below is the list I prepared for my Bible study,
but the concept is a work in progress. Life will, I am sure, continue
to show me new ways God works to help us become whole, healthy,
transformed, liberated, and empowered.

This, then, is my explanation of what I call the resurrection
principle.

Practicing resurrection . . .

. . . is keeping on when everything in your life seems to scream
for you to give up.

. . . is seeking to find where God is at work in your life, in a
relationship, or in a tough situation, and working *with* God and his
life-giving energy. In other words, it is "helping God help us."

. . . is refusing to be squashed into the boxes other people might
place around you, the ones you have made for yourself and the ones

you have outgrown, and daring to live what Mary Oliver celebrated as the "one wild and precious life" you have been given.

. . . is letting God out of the boxes we have put him in so that he has the freedom and elbow room to create something new and better in our lives.

. . . is coming to the end of your strength, your hope, your ability to take one more step, declaring "I cannot go on," and then, in the next breath, insisting "I will go on."

. . . is sitting on the ash heap of suffering, like Job, until you hear the faint whisper of God's grace saying, "Let's get up and live."

. . . is searching relentlessly for the truth about things. It is telling the truth and standing up to the lies you may have bought into or the lies other people try to convince you are true.

. . . is believing in yourself—belief in the inherent goodness of the world and a radical belief and trust in God.

. . . is living from the center of your being instead of being conformed to the image of your outer world.

. . . is waiting out the dark, perhaps thinking that you cannot bear another moment of pain, until the dawn breaks.

. . . is bearing the unbearable silence of God until you come to know that all along, God has been speaking to you—and perhaps even singing—and knowing, finally, that the only songs God knows are love songs.

. . . is enduring the seeming absence of God until finally you know for sure that there is no valley so deep that God will not go there with you, that there is no night so long that God is not with you, and that there is no silence of God—and you finally hear the steady, unrelenting heartbeat of the creator, the life-giver of the cosmos who says, "You are mine. I have carved your name on the palm of my hand. You are precious in my sight, and I will never leave you or forsake you."

. . . is believing, when all the evidence seems to contradict it, the truth in Jesus' words, "Greater is He who is in you than he who is in the world" (1 John 4:4).

... is believing in, hoping for, and trusting in the resurrection life that lives in you, even if you cannot see it.

On the day after my discussion with Martus about practicing resurrection and my idea of the resurrection principle, he came home from the church with his file folder, and we sat down again after dinner.

"I've decided that I'm going to start with the Scripture Dwain wanted and incorporate the idea of the resurrection principle," he began until I stopped him with a strong

"Wait just a minute! I thought you didn't give validity to my idea!" I protested.

He sat there a moment, and then he said, "I thought it over today. I think you are right."

"Are you conceding?" I asked him.

"No," he responded. "I am agreeing with you." Our banter about the "resurrection principle" was light-hearted, but it also made me think about how the theological systems, beliefs, and ideas that spring into the collective consciousness have come from human beings making their sometimes educated, often prejudiced, sometimes intuitive leaps of faith.

Perhaps practicing resurrection means you can open your mind to a new idea or a new way of saying an ancient truth.

Sometimes practicing resurrection means that you hold firm to what you believe to be true, even when someone important to you questions you.

For sure, practicing resurrection means I don't have to gloat.

But I do enjoy that story.

I was fortunate, getting to adulthood, and the first big loss I experienced happened when I had a miscarriage while living in Nacogdoches, Texas.

To recover from the physical and emotional toll the experience took on my body, I went on long walks every day during the chilly December afternoons. I asked a babysitter to come every day to stay with our two young daughters, who were four and one, so that I could walk the neighborhood streets under towering pine trees and often dreary skies that matched my moods. Walking has always been a good way for me to work things out in my mind and heart.

One dreary day, a memory verse from the past suddenly came to me unbidden. I don't know why that particular verse popped up from my mental archives, but I will never forget that moment the words from the Apostle Paul came to me on Appleby Sand Road. At the same moment, my sadness and depression started to lift: "If the Spirit of the Lord who raised Jesus from the dead is living in you, he who raised Christ from the dead will also give life to your mortal bodies through his Spirit who lives in you" (Rom 8:17).

As I finished my walk and headed home to my two precious little girls, the late afternoon sun had begun to slip behind the giant pine trees, but I could feel the life return to my whole body. Simply remembering that the life-giving, life-altering, life-saving presence of God was in me connected me to that Source, and I felt alive again.

I still remember the loss of my baby on that scary November day, but I also remember that moment in December when the Mystery used my memory to connect me with a verse from Romans, and how that verse then connected me to the Spirit of life within me, the resurrection principle.

Questions to Ponder

1. Practicing resurrection requires a change of mind from negativism to a faith perspective. In what ways might it be hard for you to let go of a negative point of view about yourself, another person, a world situation, or a personal problem?

2. If you can't change a situation, what might be changed about your own perspective by seeing from a different point of view, handling the situation in a more productive way, or even taking the risk to talk honestly and openly about the situation with someone you trust?

3. As you look at the description or definition of "practicing resurrection" in this chapter, what situation in your life comes to mind? Could God be calling you to a new approach to this situation?

4. Americans are tied to self-sufficiency, personal responsibility, independence, and a fierce commitment to "I'll do it myself." How do those good qualities work against us when they are carried too far or when they prevent us from letting go and letting God help?

I've never lived this day before.
   All I know to do right now is
all I have ever done before.
   I don't know how the situation
   I'm facing is going to end.
   All I have learned to expect
   is what I have seen in the past.

I'm not sure where to begin,
and so I'm just sitting here,
waiting until I know how to do
what I've never had to do before.
   Does anyone else ever feel
   scared?
Why does everyone else
look so self-confident?
   Oh, God, I am so new at this
   part of life and living.
   I don't feel like I am prepared.

I can try to figure it out,
but what if I can't? What if I fail at starting over?
Can you just give me a hint, a push, even a shove
in the direction you want me to go?

Chapter 4

KEEPING HOPE ALIVE

A friend calls coincidence "God at work, remaining anonymous"; another insists that the seeming chance of things coming together in an unusual way is no mere chance but "God's fingerprints."

Carl Jung used the term "synchronicity" to describe a simultaneous occurrence of unrelated events that have meaning for the people involved.

I love the biblical idea of *the fullness of time* when the moment is right for an event to occur, such as the birth of Jesus.

During my years of depth analysis, I learned to identify patterns of attitude, emotion, and action that, as Paul wrote in Romans 8:18-19, "made me do the very things I did not want to do and not do the things I wanted to do." Becoming more conscious of these patterns of behavior gave me more freedom and taught me to take responsibility for who I am. Through depth analysis, I came to understand what made me get stuck in my own memories and emotions and allowed me to overcome a lifetime of self-sabotaging patterns.

Through depth analysis, I also became more alert to those moments when it seemed to me that the exact thing I needed to learn, the person I needed to meet, the book I needed to read, or the experience I needed to have appeared at just the right time. I was so amazed by the frequency of such experiences that I began to keep a list in my journal. I often said I did that to *keep hope alive* and for reference when I became discouraged or disheartened, disappointed or despairing.

Often, what I have needed to take the next step of faith has come in the form of what Proverbs calls *a word fitly spoken*. A phrase, a quotation, or even a joke—and certainly a Scripture—has seemed to appear at just the right time to be a light on my path.

God does work in mysterious ways, and sometimes he uses humor.

"The rain, it falleth everywhere, on the just and the unjust fellow. But more, it seems, on the just . . . because the unjust have the just's umbrella!"

The writer Madeleine L'Engle, friend and mentor in my early days of writing, shared this rhyme while speaking at Laity Lodge Retreat Center, catching us blind-sided with her wry humor. I loved the way Madeleine could teach deep wisdom with humor.

Madeleine had her share of heartaches and tragedies, and out of her deep faith she shared generously her good, common sense; her wit; and her wisdom. My faith grew as I apprenticed myself to her. Her open mind and heart expressed themselves in open arms to those of us who were fortunate enough to cross her path and sit at her feet.

Life happens, and it sometimes happens gloriously and sometimes tragically. Sometimes the same kind of event can occur to two different people, and one person survives and thrives while the other person crumbles or even dies.

How do we account for the various responses to hardship and difficulty in human beings? What activates resilience in some but not in others?

What does faith have to do with our ability to overcome our difficulties, survive our tragedies, and bear the burdens that don't go away? What causes one person to begin again when he has lost everything or the most precious thing and another to give up and disappear into one of the many forms of oblivion available to human beings? What do you reach for when there's no longer anything there?

What can you do to keep moving forward when all that you valued most, loved most dearly, and enjoyed most happily is in the past?

Is there any difference between those of us who practice one form of religion or another and those who proclaim that there is no God?

In trial or in tribulation, is there a difference between those who are practicing Christians and those who have a positive attitude?

How are faith and one's mental attitude connected, or are they? And as for faith, don't we have to ask faith *in what* or *in whom*?

The first time I heard the phrase "keeping hope alive" was when I read it in *Forgive and Forget: Healing the Hurts We Don't Deserve* by Lewis Smedes. It captured my imagination.

Listening to Smedes lecture at Laity Lodge retreat center, I was fascinated by his stories and his wisdom but mostly by his profound humility, compassion, and gentleness. Looking back, I realize now how the spiritual grace of hope is profoundly connected with the powerful and often difficult act of forgiveness.

Keeping hope alive became a part of my quest, both in my own life and also in my work. On several occasions, I have led weekend-long retreats or given thirty-minute speeches on the theme of "Keeping Hope Alive" as a guiding principle in doing spiritual direction.

It seems to be true that we teachers and writers often teach what we want to learn, and I have lived with the awareness that the topic of keeping hope alive captivated me because of what was going on around me and with the people I love.

Now and then when I am teaching or leading a retreat, I like to ask participants to tell me what pieces of advice and life lessons they learned from their parents or grandparents. When it comes to handling heartache and loss, difficulties and disappointments, there is a wide range of pithy sayings on which people often build their whole lives:

I'm going to pick myself up, dust myself off, and start all over again!

If life hands you a lemon, make lemonade.

Grin and bear it! Bite the stick if it hurts. Don't let them know they hurt you.

Indeed, good things can come from staying strong when what we want to do is give in to weakness. Sometimes we do have to get a grip and get through a hard time. Falling apart or becoming numb only makes things harder, right?

I have no quarrel with people who tell me things like "if it is to be, it's up to me!" or try to encourage me by saying that "failure is not in falling down but in failing to get up." Goodness knows I've used those bromides on others and myself. It's the American way, isn't it?

Much good has been accomplished in this world by the power of self-will, tenacity, stubbornness, and the refusal to bend or break under the difficulties and challenges of both everyday life and the tragedies, disasters, and chaos that befall human beings. There is something to be said for the resilience of mortals who, when called upon to do more, do it longer and do it better simply to survive. They draw on strengths they didn't know they had until put to the test, accomplishing heroic feats and surviving hardship, loss, and even torture.

I bow in awe at what suffering individuals have been able to bear by faith in their own strengths. The astonishing acts of creativity, productivity, and nobility that human beings are able to accomplish in spite of limitation, loss, and difficulty are dazzling.

"The secret to getting through life is all in the attitude," an old friend told me. "If you think you can, you can. If you think you can't, that's true, too. You just have to be positive."

The "positive thinking" route is an enormous industry, generating books and recordings, motivational seminars, and huge profits for those who perpetuate the practices of a positive mental attitude. Enormous crowds flock to churches that teach and preach the principles of positive thinking, success motivation, and the idea that "it's all in the mind."

I have to agree that a positive attitude is better than a negative one, but I am also aware that authentic transformation happens only when the shadow energies, painful events, and negative thoughts that exist in all of us are brought into consciousness and respected for what they are and what they represent.

And then there are good-intentioned people who wish to cover up all that is unpleasant, unsavory, or ugly with God-talk. There are those who are so uncomfortable in the presence of suffering that the only way they can bear it is to spiritualize it or slap bumper-sticker theology on whatever hurts too much to face.

"Just trust God," a friend was told when she was diagnosed with cancer. "You know that faith can move mountains."

"God was watching over us," a stranger on television declared after her house was saved in the tornado that devastated the houses of the people across the street.

"Everything that happens is God's will, and you will understand someday," a person told a grieving parent. "God must have needed a new angel today."

Sometimes people blame God for what they themselves have done. Some take the credit for what God has done through them. Sometimes people blame God for doing one thing or not doing another, when all the time the logical consequences of their choices have led them to the situation they don't want to face.

"I would love to tell you that God helped me do this," a person told me one time, "but the truth is that I didn't ask him to help me and it doesn't really seem I needed him, does it?"

That took my breath away, but only for a second. I would love to tell you that this bold person was just teasing, but when I looked into his eyes, I saw that he was a true believer in the power of his own mind, strength, and ability.

How many ways are there to deal with pain and suffering?

Positive thinking. Blind faith or active faith in a supreme being. Grin and bear it. Drink (or eat or work or gamble) the pain away. Pretend it didn't happen; call it a euphemism or blame it on someone else. Declare every morning, "If it is to be, it's up to me." Distract yourself from the pain. Surround yourself with support and call on them to help you get through the hard part.

Does being a Christian make any difference when it comes to suffering? Does belief in Christ help us when we're hurting?

When you consider your customary way of handling stress and trauma, difficulty and despair, it may be helpful to ask yourself, "How's that working for you?"

Sometimes, all it takes is a song to reconnect you with something important.

When I was young, the song "The Impossible Dream" from the stage musical *Man of La Mancha* ignited minds and hearts with Don Quixote's quest to make the world a better place.

I was a dreamer then, too, so the song became my personal anthem. Young and optimistic, I believed in infinite possibilities of life and love, and so it was that, fortified by that song and "Climb Every Mountain" from *The Sound of Music,* I set out into the adult world to make my dreams come true.

Over time, life tempered my youthful spirit, balancing idealism with realism and pragmatism. With some losses and heartbreaks along the way, I have worked to maintain my optimism, but now and then, I've felt the grunge of cynicism and skepticism.

I don't like the feelings that accompany cynicism and skepticism. You know what they are: resentment, bitterness, jealousy, envy on good days, and disappointment, despair, depression, and hopelessness on bad days.

Those feelings are indicative that I am betraying the truths that I know to be, well, *true.* When I am in those awful pits, I know I am betraying my True Self, and, worse, I know that in those states, I am distancing myself from the Life-giver and the Source of unconditional love and unrelenting hope.

On a whim one winter, I asked for tickets to a stage production of *Man of La Mancha* for my birthday. There was probably nothing I needed more than to immerse myself in the music and the story of a man who, either by delusion or by faith, changed the lives of a group of disheartened and frightened prisoners during the Spanish Inquisition by the pursuit of his impossible dream.

At the time, I was struck by the presence of themes I'd also found in the movies I had been watching. The movie *Argo* depicts the dramatic rescue of captured Americans. *Les Miserables* portrays the tension between one character who works to keep people in bondage and another, the hero, who works for the good of the "miserable ones" for whom life had dealt cruel blows. *Lincoln* is about a man who risked his political influence and mortal life for the abolition of slavery, and *Silver Linings Playbook* focuses on two people fighting their way out of the prisons of their own minds or behavioral patterns.

> *I have set before you today life and death, blessing and curse. Therefore, choose life.*
>
> Deuteronomy 30:19

Painful to watch because of the stark reality it reveals, the award-winning *Amour* takes us into the world of aging and dying to show us the unbearable grief of loneliness and isolation at the end of life. Trapped in the inevitable, a husband and wife did, I suppose, the best they could, but my heart kept insisting, "Don't you know that there is a better way to do this?"

Over and over, I wondered what this prevailing theme about being trapped or imprisoned and the lengths to which human beings will go for freedom and hope says about the times we are in.

Could it be that collectively, we are all yearning for silver linings to dark, gray clouds?

Could it be that there is something in us that knows we are meant for freedom, intended for life, designed neither to be imprisoned—either by the chains of our own making or the tyranny of others—nor merely to survive but to thrive and flourish, to replenish the earth with our creativity and acts of common kindness and even, now and then, our acts of heroism?

It's staggering to think about how much anxiety we humans carry at this particular time in history. Who among us doesn't have his or her personal or family challenges to carry and crosses to bear? Who among us doesn't worry about our finances, our health, our safety, the future either for our own lives or for those of our loved ones?

I confess this: I often succumb to numbing my anxieties by codependency. I do that, quite simply, as pain relief.

If our personal issues were not enough, we swim in a thick soup of constant and unrelenting cultural crises. We are inundated with news that threatens our jobs, the environment, our daily traffic patterns, and our safety. In many ways, we are powerless under the control other people have over much of our daily lives.

Is it any wonder, then, that we struggle to stay positive and upbeat?

Does anyone wonder why it is easy to slide into the emotional quagmires and quicksand of cynicism and negativism or feel imprisoned by our fears?

Working my program of recovery and maintaining my spiritual practices *one day at a time* is necessary for me to stay in the flow of God's great grace and mercy, and I mean *every single day*. No exceptions.

My spiritual practices keep me centered in hope, and those practices are as necessary to the care of my soul as breathing is to my physical body. I am vigilant about those practices—at least most of the time. Those practices are, for me, my ways of *practicing resurrection.*

What I didn't realize, however, back in the winter when I asked for *Man of La Mancha* for my birthday, was just how much I needed to hear the powerful, life-affirming words of that song I'd adopted as a theme song in my youth. At the first line, I wept. (Thankfully, I didn't sob out loud!)

I didn't realize how much I'd let anxiety and cynicism creep into my life until that song activated my memories and, with them, my youthful hope and optimism. I wasn't the only one who needed to hear "The Impossible Dream," though; I heard sniffling all around me, and at the end, we rose to our feet together, strangers sitting at the Hobby Center, and gave Don Quixote a rousing and extended ovation.

Somehow, that Hobby Center became a sanctuary of grace and a holy place of hope that evening, at least for me.

Here's my biggest gift from that evening. Don Quixote is the Christ-figure in a dank and dirty prison cell, and in his fantasy, he begins relating to the other prisoners from a place of hope and faith, but he changes Aldonza's life the most.

Born in a ditch, abandoned by her mother, used and abused, Aldonza has come to accept that she is merely a victim of other people with a rough, tough exterior that she has manufactured as a defense against the pain of her life.

Don Quixote, however, sees beyond the exterior of her life. He looks beyond what seems to be true and locates in her the woman of his dreams, *Dulcinea*, and no matter how much she protests that she is Aldonza and not Dulcinea, he persists and insists that what he sees is true.

I did almost cry out loud at the end when Aldonza, brought to her knees in grief over the death of Don Quixote, declares to another prisoner who called her Aldonza, "I am not Aldonza; I am *Dulcinea!*"

Experience has taught me that when we are trying to recover from an addiction, heal through a loss, make personal changes, or discern where and how and sometimes whether God is at work in us, a good sponsor, a spiritual director, a priest, or a therapist is an instrument of hope. An objective person who has our spiritual growth and our personal welfare in mind sees our failures and our character defects but doesn't see them as all of who we are.

A wise and sensitive guide recognizes our duplicities and deceptions, our raw, rough, awful places, and does not gloss over them. A person who has done his or her own inner work is able to hold those things about the directee, the patient, the parishioner in the right perspective, looking beyond them and refusing to accept that this is all that person is. A good and caring guide holds a vision of who we are, created in the very image of God, for us until we can accept it for ourselves.

Someone who can listen and provide a steady, calm presence is invaluable when we are forced to give up hope, to yield our desires to the realities we cannot escape, to put away optimism and feel-good-ism and face the things we cannot change.

For those of us within the Christian community, there is nothing like someone who is a priest to us, mediating the very mercy, grace, forgiveness, and love of God to us in portions we can accept and believe.

For those of us within the Christian community, a caring listener and willing instrument of love has the opportunity to be Christ to us, believing that somewhere in us, perhaps hidden under layers of guilt, shame, and self-doubt, there is Dulcinea, the person we were created to be.

One of the ways we can practice resurrection is to be priests to each other.

Needless to say, I bought the soundtrack to the show.

What do you think? Is it ever too late to dream the impossible dream of wholeness, resurrection, sobriety, serenity?

Is the cost too heavy to walk into hell for a heavenly cause?

I suppose each of us has to answer that question for ourselves; however, I am asking God for the radical courage to keep pursuing the impossible dream of a better world, a safer world, a world in which all of us have a chance to be redeemed from the prisons we are in and set free to live the abundant life we've been designed to live.

Sometimes letting go of the old, egocentric self feels like a cruci-fixion. I get that. But new life is possible once we are willing to let the old self—the false, constricted, and miserable self—die.

New life is the whole story of resurrection, and there's no time like the present to claim the resurrection for yourself.

Questions to Ponder

1. Who has been Christ to you, mediating radical acceptance and empowering love to you?

2. Have you dared to put yourself in the presence of someone who sees you with the eyes of grace?

3. Has anyone ever called you by your real name, only to have you insist on being called by the name that limits you, holds you hostage?

4. What would be different in your life if you could accept your True Self as the operative self and leave the imprisoned self behind?

5. Who has struggled with you when you have to let hope die? Who has hung in there with you while you struggled to keep hope alive?

I think I am at a crossroads, God.
I think this is it.
    I can either keep on going down
    the same old road that keeps
    taking me to the places I don't
    want to go . . .
or I can risk my life
and take a chance on hope
and hope that maybe there is
life on the other side
of this place where I
am, where I don't
want to linger.
    I've been at this crossroads before.
    I know what it's like to stand here
        too long and lose my nerve.
This time, it feels like it's time.
I'm going to trust you, God,
while I reach into my heart for strength
    I don't yet feel
and hope I'm not sure is there.
        I'm willing.
Would you please hold on while I let go?

Chapter 5

GOD AT WORK IN ALL THINGS

Recently, on a sunny day in early spring, I walked into the Holocaust Museum of Houston to participate in the first of four one-day workshops on family systems.

From the moment I walked in, I felt as if the word *hope* was emblazoned on something wherever I looked. Hope was on the program guide for the current exhibit, on T-shirts and mugs, and on one of the ubiquitous plastic wristbands people wear to identify with one cause or another. Stamped on the green wristbands available at the Holocaust museum were these words: "Hope is greater than hate. #StandWithHope." Scattered about were butterflies made by children as part of the Butterfly Project, and I also found a book about that project.

In the back of the museum is a statue of the biblical character of Job and a stunning art piece of butterflies flying off the pages of a book.

In the process of completing this book, I was stunned in those first few minutes by the presence of the word *hope* in every direction, but when I walked to the back of the lobby and out into the Eric Alexander Garden of Hope, a garden dedicated to the 1.5 million children who died in the Holocaust, I moved in silence.

In front of me was a large granite wall inscribed with these words attributed to a sixteen-year-old Jewish girl, Alena Synková:

Though there is anguish
deep in my soul—
What if I must search for you forever?
I must not lose faith,
I must not lose hope.

It is easier to think of the children who died in the Holocaust as nameless, and so I include this young girl's name as a tribute to her personhood. I confess that it is easier to think of those who died as a mass of humanity, and harder to think of each one *as a human being made in the very image of God*, named by a parent who bestowed her name with hope.

In the Garden of Hope is a 1942 World War II rail car like those used to carry millions of Jews to their deaths, the kind I have seen only in movies. I confess that I didn't want to look inside, but I did. There are quotations around the museum that must be absorbed, but the idea I brought home with me that day was the idea of *remembering*. I felt a call to remember where we have been that was wrong or evil, not to dwell in the horrors but to avoid repeating the past. I felt a call to remember in order to make the path ahead a better one, to make freedom ring for others, to keep hope alive so that there can be a future for ourselves and others.

The call to remembrance, interspersed throughout the museum with the word *hope*, was a vivid reminder that hope flourishes in and through those of us who are able to carry both the terrible and the wonderful memories of the past as a foundation for the future.

One of the most wonderful moments of my life was when I watched the light of understanding break across the face of my eighty-five-year-old father only a few weeks before he died. I'll never forget his laughter at himself as he gave up a long-held interpretation of a particular Scripture and a long-held, unexamined stance about the role of women in the church in order to allow the fresh breezes of new understanding to take their place.

"How would a woman know she was called by God?" my father asked my sisters and me.

"Daddy, how would a man know?" my older sister asked, and with that question a lifelong understanding shifted for my father, a Baptist minister, and his whole face lit up.

"Well, of course . . . of course!" he answered, laughing with the joy of a child who has made a new discovery. For the rest of the day, he periodically chuckled quietly to himself as he watched his three daughters and pondered his new consciousness.

He had, after all, told us we could do anything we wanted to do and anything God called us to do. The former was a bit of an illusion, but the latter was a firmly held belief, and both were intended to encourage us to become all that we were intended to become.

This was the man who, with the same laughter of delight, responded to my questions about how the world began by saying, "Oh, that is mystery!"

Instead of shaming me for questioning long-held tenets of faith and daring to consider that there were interpretations of the first eleven chapters of Genesis other than what I had learned in Sunday school as a child, my father gave me permission both to question those interpretations and traditions related to the Scriptures and to hold and embrace the wonder of mystery. My father made it permissible not to have to know things that are beyond human knowing; it was my father who taught me to have reverence for mystery.

Isn't it the resurrection principle alive and at work that made my father change his mind and see things with new eyes when he was an old man?

Isn't it the resurrection principle that gave some of us within my religious tradition the patience and stamina—and faith and hope—to believe that at some point, the restrictive systems with which we had grown up would change?

The problem in keeping hope alive is that fulfillment, the reaching of an important goal, the pursuit of a big dream, the correction of a societal or religious wrong can take so long, and we get weary. We get discouraged, but that doesn't have to mean we have lost our way or our hope; it may mean simply that we are weary and need to rest.

An early mentor in the beginning of my adult pilgrimage of faith
suggested that it is good now and then, but especially when you have
lost your way, to go back to the
basics. A long-time practitioner of
the Twelve Steps of Recovery, she
taught me that when I am confused
or anxious, it is helpful to ground
myself in what she called *first
things*. That wise woman told me
that all of us occasionally have to
return to the beginnings of things,
the foundations, the first building
blocks.

> *In the beginning, God
> made Adam and Eve,
> male and female . . . .
> God looked over every-
> thing he had made; it
> was good, so very good.*
>
> Genesis 1:27, 28

"We put *first things first*," she told me, and I was to learn that the
well-used slogan has many layers of meaning.

As a child, I learned Psalm 56:3: "When I am afraid, I will trust
in you." The importance of that childhood guidance was both the
simple affirmation and the lesson to go to the Bible when I was
afraid, grief stricken, or confused.

As an adult, I learned to go back to the basic teachings of Jesus,
sometimes bypassing the traditions and even the doctrines of various
expressions of Christianity to recover the vision of the early church,
all recorded in the Bible. In my pilgrimage, I had to unlearn some
things from childhood that were purely cultural—and they were
sometimes prejudicial. Always, still, I am inspired to reexamine
misinterpretations of Scripture and take a new look with fresh eyes,
new information, and an open mind.

Those misunderstandings of what God was trying to commu-
nicate to human beings, either as individuals or as the church, can
be interpreted as the results of our failures and failings, our blind
spots and biases, and our perfectly natural but often constricting
prejudices.

On the other hand, could it also be said that we must wrestle
with truth in order to understand it? Without that struggle, does
theology become mere indoctrination, spoon-fed to unthinking
people? Doesn't God give us the abilities to reason and wonder, to

agree and disagree, to dialogue and debate with big ideas, deep truths, and unfathomable mysteries perhaps to keep us from the arrogance of believing that we hold *The Truth*?

When we, the people who form the conflict-ridden church, get discouraged by our fusses and schisms, it is helpful to go to some of the stories of the early church, both those recorded in the New Testament and those we can read in church history. There we can find principles that can help us dig ourselves out of the holes we have dug with ignorance or stubbornness, willfulness or neglect. There we can also glean comfort from the fact that God is still available to us as presence and action to help us find our way.

In 664 there was a gathering of church leaders in what has been called the Synod of Whitby. Meeting in Northumbria, the synod was to address the differences in style between two spiritual worldviews.

The Celtic mission remembered John as the beloved disciple who leaned against Jesus at the Last Supper. John had become an image of the practice of listening for the heartbeat of God at the heart of life.

Our spirits were made for hope the way our hearts were made to love and our brains were made to think and our hands were made to make things. Our hearts are drawn to hope as an eagle is drawn to the sky.

—Lewis Smedes

The Roman mission, on the other hand, argued for the authority of Peter, who had become the symbol of outward unity and faithful action. This perspective favored listening for God in the ordained teaching and life of the church. Oswy, the king of Northumbria who had called the gathering, decided in favor of the Roman mission, and so the Roman perspective or worldview became the authorized religion of the land, while the Celtic mission began its formal decline.

Orthodoxy often wins not because it is right but because it is more powerful, for good or for ill.

One of the primary features of Celtic spirituality was its focus on the goodness of creation and the presence of God in all of life. One of my favorite beliefs of Celtic spirituality is that when you look into the face of a newborn baby, you are looking into the face of God. Having come fresh from God, infants were seen as special manifestations of God. Poet William Wordsworth said, "We come, streaming trails of Glory . . . ."

I have told many times the story of the little boy with his newborn sister, asking to be alone with her. Trying to ease the pain of the fall from the position of only child to older brother, the parents agreed, but they stayed near the doorway to watch and listen.

The small boy pulled his stool over to the baby's bassinet, climbed up on it, and, leaning over the infant, said, "Tell me, little sister, what heaven is like—I have almost forgotten."

Because the Roman way won, Celtic spirituality went underground but continued to flow along beneath the surface of the accepted ways of Rome. In the last twenty years, especially under the teaching and work of John Phillip Newell, there has been a resurgence of interest in earth-centered, nature-affirming spirituality and a movement away from the tight attachment to doctrine, laws, and rituals.

Within this resurgence of interest in Celtic spirituality has arisen a return to the valuing of women and of feminine strengths within the culture. In American culture, that resurgence has been met with a powerful pushback from a patriarchal, unbalanced culture. Old ways die hard, and the belief that "sin came into the world through Eve" has held firm.

In an editorial in the *Baptist Standard*, the Texas news source, editor Marv Knox asked, "How do evangelicals enable 'locker room talk' about women?" (See baptiststandard.com/classifieds/23-opinion/editorials/19592-editorial-how-do-evangelicals-enable-locker-room-talk-about-women.) Addressing the shocking words and behavior of presidential candidate Donald Trump, Knox said that the "secondary surprise is how many evangelical leaders are unable to condemn Trump and distance themselves from him."

Knox observed that this problem stems from deep theological roots, growing from Old Testament patriarchy. "Evangelicals excel at pointing to the earliest passages of Genesis and insisting all people possess value because all people are created in God's image," he wrote. That point of view is certainly consistent with the view of Celtic spirituality, but it is at odds with the idea that we are all born in original sin and destined to carry that dark stain with us, often even after we have accepted Jesus as personal savior.

An obvious example of the disconnection between the avowed adherence to the idea that we are all "made in God's image" and what is actually practiced both at home and within the church is the way females are treated. Knox continued, "So, no matter how many times they [evangelicals] tell their daughter, 'God made you, and you can be anything God wants you to be,' they don't mean it. Girls and women have their limits." (Matthew Fox lays out the differences in these two ways of seeing life and human beings in his book *Original Blessing*.)

The strength of the John tradition, the Celtic way, is that it produces a spirituality that sees God in the whole of life and regards all things as interrelated. In all creation, and in all the people of creation, the light of God is there to be seen. John's way of seeing makes room for an open encounter with the Light of life wherever it is to be found. It is a tradition that is celebrative, nature loving, joyous.

The strength of the Peter tradition, the Roman way, is that doctrine is firm and contained within the four walls of the church. It gives boundaries, traditions, sacraments, rites, rituals, and canon law. It is a rock, a place of security and shelter, and it gives us a "house of prayer" where we can turn for truth and guidance.

If we can possibly combine the best parts of both perspectives, we will have a more balanced spirituality and a broader worldview.

As a lifelong active participant in a local community of faith, I am sometimes asked if I have "seen it all." I have watched the body of Christ assailed from without by the religio-political movement of the past thirty years, the rise of fundamentalism, entertainment religion, the surge of televangelism in the 1990s and the subsequent scandals among religious celebrities. I have seen the move away from denominationalism to independent churches, mega-churches, and churches that are formed not so much about a common love and commitment to Christ as about a common political stance. I look back on the story of Adam and Eve in the Garden of Eden and shake my head at their simple defiance, wanting to be like God and thinking that eating what God had forbidden might give them that power.

I won't presume to say I have seen it all. I can say, however, that I have seen a lot. In seeing a lot, I shake my head at how hard God has had to work to reveal to us his love and his mercy, his provision and his power on our behalf.

Again and again I come back to the belief that the real problem for us is that God created us with the amazing gift (and sometimes unbearable burden) of the power to choose. I cannot answer the philosophers' big, convoluted questions about free will, but I do know that when we look at God's original intent, returning to the principle of looking at first things, we can see that when he gave Adam and Eve the instruction not to eat of the fruit of the tree of knowledge, that instruction implied that they might obey God or they might defy God.

You know the story. Eve led the way, following the goad of the serpent, which seems to signify

> *And we rejoice in the hope of the glory of God. Not only so, but we rejoice also in our sufferings because we know that suffering produces perseverance, perseverance, character, and character, hope. And hope does not disappoint us because God has poured out his love into our hearts by the Holy Spirit, whom he has given us.*
>
> Romans 5:2b-5

the part of creation that is instinctual, close to the ground, earthy. I suspect that all of us humans carry within us those energies and that those energies are resources we can use for good or for ill. Left unacknowledged, those capacities can destroy us. Acknowledged, recognized, owned, and accepted, the instinctual parts of our human nature can help us survive and even thrive.

Eve ate the fruit. Adam ate the fruit. And then God showed up, and just for a taste of fruit, history took another turn. Instantly, the eyes of these two humans were opened, which can be interpreted as the dawn of consciousness that sometimes we in my religious culture might define as coming to the age of accountability.

However you interpret that act of Adam and Eve and whether you see it as literal or figurative, the important thing to know is that the first manifestation of separation from God, represented here by defiance of God, is the impulse to hide from God.

Perhaps our defense mechanisms and our self-consciousness are fig leaves we construct to hide ourselves from God and others. Maybe the masks we wear, our projections of our own sin onto others, our denial and avoidance of facing ourselves are all the pitiful but powerful fig leaves we put on, hoping others won't see us as we are, naked and vulnerable.

This story is called "The Fall," and yet sometimes I think about what might have happened to Adam and Eve if they had stayed in the garden, naked and in complete union with the Creator. Sometimes I wonder if humankind had to make choices that would take them away from God in order to return to God.

Love, I heard, isn't really love if you aren't free *not* to love. You aren't free to stay in a relationship, I understand, if you aren't also free to go. And yet, wouldn't it have been so much easier if God had not made us quite so free?

"Wouldn't you say she was a woman submissive to her husband?" someone asked, and I struggled with what to say, whether to speak what I thought was the truth or to go along with the answer the questioner wanted.

In our traditional culture and in the particular situation I was asked about, it is sometimes hard to know whether a woman's behavior is submission or coercion. Is a child who is perfectly behaved well trained or afraid? Is the perfect little girl wanting to please, or is she afraid of what might happen if she isn't perfect? It's hard to know, sometimes, especially from the outside looking in.

And what does all of this have to do with *practicing resurrection*?

As the story goes, God ordered Adam and Eve out of the garden. He also told them how things were going to be out there, away from home, away from him. The man would have to work and the woman would have pain in childbirth, and the curious mind in me wonders if God's words were *descriptive* or *prescriptive* of how things were going to be.

Are we punished more *by* our sins or *for* them?

However you interpret that dismissal from the Garden of Eden, the redemptive activity of God can be seen in the very beginning of his relationship with human beings. Even as God had to send Adam and Eve out into the world, that resurrection principle is seen in a tender detail that is usually overlooked in the retelling of this sacred story.

God, creator and source of all that is, becomes seamstress in this story and makes for Adam and Eve coverings so that they will not be ashamed (Gen 3:21). Even as God sent Adam and Eve out of the garden, he clothed them. It seems to me that this small detail can be interpreted as God's protecting his creation, but can't it also be interpreted as the beginning of an ongoing process of God's redemptive love? Isn't this tender act a foreshadowing of God's covering of our sinful state when we walk away, distancing ourselves from him and thereby subjecting ourselves to all kinds of manifestations of our rebellion, defiance, and the need to be god?

Could we see the covering of clothing as a symbol of God's constant presence with us? And isn't it likely that within Adam and Eve God planted hope that would keep them moving forward?

There are times in my life when I have bumped into a wall of failure. There have been times when I've been discouraged, wanted to quit, change directions, or go back to a more comfortable place or time like the Garden of Eden. Sometimes I have been caught in the vise of needing to choose between two alternatives I did not want. At other times, I have simply wanted to make a choice or do something, anything, in order to feel better, but I have learned that if I can manage the stress of the moment, the choice I must make is one that is progressive and life-giving and not regressive and death-dealing.

There are times in my life when I have fallen from grace in my own eyes, made choices that took me away from what I knew was the right path and away from an awareness of God. There have been times when I have known the right thing to do but have chosen—either willfully, carelessly, or arrogantly—to do the wrong thing.

The memory of Adam and Eve, clothed by God even as they exited the Garden of Eden, reminds me that I do not walk alone. And it gives me hope.

In the difficult times when I feel stuck and unable to move, I remember that God is still present and at work in my circumstances and in me. Hope itself, present within my heart, gives me what I need to act or to wait, to push through the pain, the difficulty, or the paralysis.

God has given us the gift of hope to keep us going on our uncertain journey.

—Lewis Smedes

In his book *Keeping Hope Alive*, Lewis Smedes says that hope is bred in our bones. He writes, "One way or the other, all people hunger for hope because our Maker made us to live by hope."

My mother often said that "love covers a multitude of sins."

When I moved away from close friends with whom I had shared heartaches and victories, struggles and joyful moments, my friends gave me a painting of colorful outer clothing—coats, capes, and jackets—hanging on a coat rack. "We are covering you as you go, Jeanie," they told me, and I cried over the pain of leaving them.

Every time I look at that painting, I remember my friends who covered me with their prayers, their love, their letters and calls. They helped me as I made the painful journey of letting go of the familiar, warm, close weekly association with them and went out into a strange, new world. That painting gave me courage, reminded me of the love of friends, and helped me let go of what had been and open my heart to what was to come.

As the children of Israel tried to make their way in freedom instead of bondage, God spoke words of guidance to them, words that I now understand as guidance in accessing the resurrection principle in everyday life, and especially in trouble or trauma. Those words are found in Deuteronomy 30:19, and they form a foundation for my ability to practice resurrection: "I have set before you today life and death, blessing and curse. Therefore, choose life."

If sin is defined as separation from God, we act as if we are lords and ladies of the universe in an infinite number of ways. We can call sins of action missing the mark, going our own way, or defying the boundaries God has set, but whatever we call them reflects separation from God.

However you see this ancient story from Genesis, it contains a paradox: Adam and Eve and all people who were to be born would experience separation from God, but God is never separate from us. The name *Emmanuel*, God-with-us, is not an accidental name. It's a name filled with stunning reassurance.

God is everywhere. Sometimes we may forget that truth. We may not believe it or trust it, but God's presence is a given in our lives. God is not dependent on our believing in him, and neither does he need us to trust him in order for him to be trustworthy. God, the source of all that is, is with us and at work, attempting to bring about good.

I've learned that if you believe it, you will see it. And sometimes, even if you don't believe it, even reject God, he may strip the blinders from your eyes and shock you with his presence and shake your foundations with his love. I know this because I have witnessed the resurrection power at work in human beings. I know this because I have experienced God's love when I thought he had abandoned me.

I believe in God's working for good even when it takes an unbearably long time for human beings to accomplish what is right and just and fair. I believe because I must believe: it is hope in God that keeps my dreams alive and gives me stamina and perseverance to pursue them.

In the beginning was God. Always, the God whose name is love is the foundation of life, and it is God's love that is the energy, impetus, and spirit who activates the resurrection principle in us, often when we think there is nothing but a dead end ahead.

> Don't you know anything? Haven't you been listening?
> God doesn't come and go. God lasts.
> He's the Creator of all you can see or imagine.
> He doesn't get tired, doesn't pause to catch his breath.
> And he knows everything, inside and out.
> He energizes those who get tired;
> gives fresh strength to dropouts.
> For even young people in their prime stumble and fall.
> But those who wait upon God get fresh strength.
> They spread their wings and soar like eagles.
> They run and don't get tired.
> They walk and don't lag behind. (Isa 40:28-31, *The Message*)

Isaiah knew about keeping hope alive. And he knew that it is the very nature of God to nourish and nurture the spark of hope that seems to be planted within us.

I wear my green wristband from the Holocaust Museum as I write these words as a remembrance of Synková, who was determined not to lose hope.

Questions to Ponder

1. If someone asked you who God is to you, what would you say?

2. If someone asked you who you are to God, what would you say?

3. Do you really believe that God is with you, as near as your breath?

4. What connection is there between your concept of God and your sense of hope?

❋ ❋ ❋

If I accept the premise that you are at work in all things, God,
  how do I recognize what you are doing?
If it is true that you really are Emmanuel, God-with-us,
  how can I sense your presence?
    If my job is to discern what you are doing,
    where you are at work,
what you seem to be bringing about, please give me just enough
light
to take the next step.
Or maybe you could whisper my name
or whistle in a way I would recognize.
    If I accept the premise that you are at work
    in my life, in this situation, in the world,
    sharpen my sense, please,
so that I don't follow the
wrong signal down the
wrong path.
    God whose name is Emmanuel,
    I know you as Redeemer, too . . .
and you know my intention.
If I get it wrong, your love will turn me around.

Chapter 6

MEANT FOR PILGRIMAGE

It was a visual image so simple that a child could grasp it and so powerful that it has returned to me countless times since my West Texas friend Travis Perry explained the power of prayer to me.

Sitting in our small living room in San Angelo in a Yokefellow Spiritual Growth Group, Trav had listened intently to a conversation about the week's topic. The book we were using was *Prayer Can Change Your Life*, but the approach of authors Parker and St. Johns was different from the typical approach to prayer that all of us had learned in church. Finally, Trav spoke up.

"It is so simple, prayer is, and we make it so complicated. God's presence is everywhere and we just have to access it."

We all sat there in perplexed silence, and then Trav pointed to an electrical outlet and said, "It's this simple: praying is plugging in to the power. No, we can't see it, but we all know that the power is in that outlet."

This image worked for me primarily because I love the image of our relationship with God defined by Jesus in John 15 as like the relationship of the vine to the branches. The life of God flows into us as naturally and as consistently as the life force of the vine flows into the branches, producing the fruit that is inherent in the vine.

We can't see electricity, except in lightning and occasional sparks, and we can't see God, and we can't see love—but we observe the manifestations of God and love.

I see the activity of God more in retrospect, but now and then, the holiness of God breaks through my conscious mind and sends chills over my physical body. Sometimes I feel the tug of compassion in an almost physical way in my heart, and now and then the presence of great joy or deep sorrow seem to come from God to awaken me to the moment or to the human condition.

My mother's term "to be under conviction" could be interpreted as the nudging of the Holy Spirit to make me see things more clearly, become accountable for a word badly spoken or a deed that hurt someone. However, an overactive guilt complex or an overzealous desire to please another person may have more to do with one's relationship with early authority figures, teachers and parents than it does the work of the Holy Spirit.

Always do what you are afraid to do.

—Ralph Waldo Emerson

Indeed, the Holy Spirit does make us aware of what we have done that is wrong, but increasingly, I understand the work of God-within has more to do with our being drawn by the love of God into a deeper intimacy with God. We are aware of our sin or mistakes not so we can beat ourselves up with shame and guilt, but so we can receive the mercy and grace of God, who does not want us to injure ourselves or others and who longs to forgive us and help us learn how to live in freedom and in love.

Discernment is one of the gifts of the process of becoming conscious, and discernment helps us learn the difference between guilt and shame complexes that keep us stuck and those moments of awakening that lead us to freedom.

Becoming aware of one's inner life is an ongoing process, and it takes practice in listening to distinguish the Spirit of God within from the same old inner tapes of a lifetime speaking to us. Being tuned in to the activity of God within one's inner life and being watchful of the acts of God in the outer world are gifts that enable us to work with God to bring about good.

Because learning to listen and discern is so important, I practice Centering Prayer, the method of contemplative prayer taught by author and Cistercian monk Fr. Thomas Keating, founder of Contemplative Outreach, and Fr. William Menninger. In the practice of Centering Prayer, we know that our prayer word is not magic—but neither is it meaningless. The sacred word, or prayer word, is intended to give consent to the practice and presence of God within us. As Trav put it, the prayer word we choose is the means by which we enter the silence and "plug in" to the power of God.

In my life, it is the plugging in, the daily practice of Centering Prayer, that has moved me from experience to experience, heartbreak to peace, sorrow to joy, guilt and shame to forgiveness, and fear to love. It is the work of what Thomas Keating calls "the Divine Therapist," who acts below my conscious level, beyond my ego, and deep within my heart in the places I cannot see, moving my life forward, day by day, to meaning and purpose that I could never have imagined in that small living room gathering of our Yokefellow group.

In 1998 on a vacation to San Francisco, I insisted on a visit to Grace Cathedral so that I could see the labyrinth I had learned about during my training at the Spiritual Direction Institute in Houston. My travel buddies accommodated my wish, but frankly, the visit frustrated me and perhaps them.

Upon our arrival at Grace Cathedral that spring morning, we found the labyrinth crowded with people, both tourists and serious walkers. I wasn't informed enough about the labyrinth at the time, and the others were not interested in a circular piece of carpet shaped like something they didn't understand. I had expected a quieter, more contemplative experience in the cathedral, but my friends were impatient to get on with our sightseeing. I left with my curiosity and longing still in high gear.

On the way out of the cathedral, I stopped at a rack by the large doors and picked up a flyer about the labyrinth workshops and facilitator training in Chartres, France, took it home with me, and sent an email to be put on the mailing list for the Chartres pilgrimages.

For thirteen years, I read every word of the brochures that came to me, and for thirteen years, I longed to make the pilgrimage to Chartres, learn about the labyrinth, and become trained to lead labyrinth workshops. And for thirteen years, I discarded the brochures with a silent prayer along the lines of "maybe someday." Such a pilgrimage seemed out of reach for me until, one day in 2010, my friend Carole Keating brought me a Pilgrim's Badge from Chartres, placed it in my hand, and said, "It is time for you to go."

In 2011, I made my first pilgrimage to the grand cathedral in Chartres, France, to participate in a labyrinth workshop led by Lauren Artress. It was a big and costly step to take, and the journey was the fulfillment of a longtime dream.

The journey from Paris to Chartres, everything I learned in the workshops in the eleven days I spent in the ancient cathedral there, the wisdom and knowledge of Lauren Artress, and the exquisite candlelit labyrinth walk in the cathedral expanded my mind and heart in ways I am still discovering now, years later. I knew I was changed, but precisely how I was changed continues to unfold from the inside out.

That pilgrimage marked a turning point in my life. Though I didn't fully see it at the time, it marked the end of one chapter of my life and the beginning of another. It was an experience that allowed me to grasp the power of Wendell Berry's poem and the words of the last line, *practice resurrection.*

"I'm satisfied," I told my family. "It was wonderful. It was the experience of a lifetime, and I won't need to go again. It was a perfect pilgrimage in every way."

Never expecting to have the privilege or opportunity of returning to that sacred place, I was content. In May 2016, though, I made my way to Chartres again for my third pilgrimage, and while I am content with having experienced those pilgrimages, I still long to return.

The desire to go on pilgrimage is filled with surprise. I never know what I will experience, what breakthrough of understanding I might have, what solution to a problem I might discover, or, sometimes, what difficulty I might face that contains within it the seed of new understanding or of the direction my journey is to take.

On this most recent pilgrimage to Chartres and then to Assisi in the following week, I made peace with a part of myself that I have felt guilty about for most of my adult life. All of a sudden, in a *kairos* moment—that moment when a coincidence or synchronicity stops you in your tracks and points you to the awareness of God's breaking through ordinary time to reveal something you need to know.

Celtic spirituality teaches us to be aware of "thin places," when the veil between heaven and earth is thin and you know that what you have perceived or experienced is, indeed, holy. Those *kairos* moments are times you look back on and know that "indeed, God was in this place" (see Gen 28:16).

I have often wondered at the strange, stirring desire that has prompted me to journey to this particular cathedral so many times. More generally, I've struggled with my guilt over what I perceived to be my lack of satisfaction. I returned from my first Chartres pilgrimage content, but the feeling was replaced over time with a fervent yearning to return. I was blessed to go that first time and blessed further by my second trip. I should be satisfied. Sitting on a plane to France yet again, I felt guilt for wanting to "ask, seek, knock" in my response to my yearning for more. It was only on this third trip that I began to let go of the guilt. I yearn for Chartres, for this physical place where God has changed my spirit so dramatically; and I know that God has designed us for growth.

Long before my third pilgrimage to Chartres to walk the labyrinth in the floor of the cathedral, long before I had ever heard of Phil Cousineau or Lauren Artress or other speakers from whose deep wells I had been privileged to drink in workshops sponsored by Veriditas, I sat with my friend Mary Ellen Hartje in a favorite booth at the Crystal Confectionary in San Angelo, Texas.

Mary Ellen had introduced me to the work of Joseph Campbell and his hero's journey, to Bill Moyers and his fascinating PBS interviews titled "The Power of Myth," and we were talking once again about the

Go to a land that I will show you . . . .

Genesis 12:1

mystery and wonder of "the journey" of life. Both of us had discovered the idea of life as journey, journey as destination, and the difference between a trip and a pilgrimage. As we talked, our understanding deepened.

Caught up in the enthusiasm of our conversation, I asked, "Why isn't everyone on a journey?"

I had not thought of that conversation in years, but as I sat in the meeting room at Maison St. Yves, suddenly, something Phil Cousineau said sparked my memory, and in a *kairos* moment, I was both sitting in my chair in the lecture in Chartres and remembering the intensity in Mary Ellen's face as she grabbed my hand and said, "Jeanie, some people don't even know there is a journey!"

I was stunned. I knew that what Mary Ellen was saying was true, but in a way, I didn't want to know that. I wanted to believe that everyone yearned to develop to their highest potential, and I also wanted to believe that everyone shared with me the prayer of Ignatius that is sung with such exuberance in the musical *Godspell*:

> Day by day, oh, dear Lord, three things I pray
> To see thee more clearly
> Love thee more dearly
> Follow thee more nearly, day by day

Mary Ellen and had I sat at the confectionary in silence, contemplating the largeness of life and the joys of discovering. My naiveté took a nosedive, and I was more than a little embarrassed at my idealism, but it was my limited understanding of the world that needed to be expanded. I grew up thinking that someone different from me was a Methodist. I thought the word *God* meant the same thing to everyone else as it did to me.

Never could I have imagined the world of 2016, the wide and rich diversity of my world, the places I would go or the people I would meet.

It was there in Chartres, France, in one of Phil Cousineau's lectures on the art of pilgrimage and the hero's journey, that I suddenly realized my hunger for pilgrimage, my longing to experience even deeper depths of God's presence, and my yearning to ask and seek and knock on the door of mystery are not signs of dissatisfaction or discontent at all. I am, at the same time, deeply satisfied and content with life and also infinitely curious and unceasingly drawn to experience the largeness of life.

My desire to learn more about God and to experience the presence of God in new ways is an expression of the power of hope within me. Just as God called Abraham to go to a place he would show him, and just as human history is full of pilgrims on journeys to sacred sites, spiritual pilgrimage is one of the ways I practice resurrection.

I don't know if I would ever turn down another pilgrimage, for it seems that the call to pilgrimage is calling to me. Mary Oliver expresses what is in my heart in these lines from "When Death Comes":

When it's over, I want to say: all my life
I was a bride married to amazement.
I was a bridegroom, taking the world into my arms.
When it's over, I don't want to wonder
if I have made of my life something particular, and real.
I don't want to find myself sighing and frightened or full of argument.
I don't want to end up having visited this world.

Looking back at that moment with Mary Ellen from the vantage point of Chartres, I saw that introducing the idea of life as pilgrimage and the hero's journey would be the compelling call each of us would carry in us from that point on. Mary Ellen would spend the intervening years introducing that idea to college students as she taught literature at Angelo State University, and I would spend them attempting to inspire and encourage others to take a spiritual journey.

Pilgrimage—the journey of faith that deepens your awareness of God's presence and activity in your life—is an ancient practice of seekers of God. A pilgrimage, however, does not have to be to a retreat center or to a cathedral in Chartres; it can happen in one's own home or hometown. A monk born in the seventeenth century, Brother Lawrence framed his entire life as a pilgrimage, and he taught us to practice the presence of God as we do the most mundane things, as he did in the monastery where he peeled potatoes.

In an airport on the way home from France, I spotted a T-shirt with a Tolkein quote on the front: *All who wander are not lost.*

The young woman wearing the shirt saw me staring at those words, and so I smiled at her. She smiled back, and a sparkle of recognition flashed momentarily between two strangers. I like to think that we both knew that we had found another pilgrim on the journey called life. Maybe she just liked the color of the T-shirt.

I began my writing career as a writer of Sunday school curriculum for adolescents and as a columnist for the *San Angelo Standard Times.* As life unfolded, I began teaching Bible studies to adults, always with the intention of connecting people with God and with each other through spiritual practices and principles that would affect the quality of their everyday lives.

My teaching style reflects my belief that spirituality and spiritual practice need to enrich and affect one's personal life in practical ways. It has never been enough for me to spend an hour in a worship service and count that as "following Jesus." As I see our life with God, it's a 24/7

> *You enter the forest at the darkest point, where there is no path. Where there is a way or path, it is someone else's path. You are not on your own path. If you follow someone else's way, you are not going to realize your potential.*
>
> —Joseph Campbell,
> *The Hero's Journey:*
> *Joseph Campbell on His Life's Work*

arrangement. I am not in it for the guarantee that I will go to heaven when I die; I want to know that God is with me here, now, in this present moment, and that what I do between now and death matters.

Over twenty-five years of teaching a Bible study for women at River Oak Baptist Church, I have developed the pattern of choosing a theme and then tracing that theme through the Bible, starting in the Old Testament and continuing at least through the life of Jesus.

I've had a practice of waiting until a theme has come to me through my personal study of the Bible, and then I start building my study on that slender thread throughout the Bible. For example, last year I taught a study I titled "True Freedom" in which I traced the idea of the liberating power of God throughout the Scriptures. This year, I'm teaching a study I've titled "Water into Wine: Mystery, Miracles, and Meaning for Everyday Pilgrims." My book *Fierce Love: Radical Measures for Desperate Times* was written from a yearlong study, as well as others of my books.

In a sense, my entire writing career has been a journey with ups and downs, fulfillment and frustration. Stretching to articulate both my outward and inward life pilgrimage in words that encourage or provide some support and nurture for others' journeys has given my life great meaning. Each book, in fact, could be seen as a journey within my larger pilgrimage, and each book unfolds in ways I hadn't imagined, as surely as if I were walking one of the pilgrimages in Europe.

I've said that I test my ideas with the savvy, faithful women on Thursday mornings, and if those ideas pass the TMBS test, they get to go into a book. In fact, as I write the lessons each week and as the study unfolds within the context of my dialogue with the women in this study, we stay open to what we discover. Our conversations together about the theme, the questions, and the comments that emerge from the group guide the journey as we step out into the unknown and journey together to understand a bit more about what it means to be a follower of Christ, a pilgrim, a seeker.

It has become clear to me that the journey motif that is found widely in literature, and especially in the Bible, is a powerful archetype for all cultures, and it has been so for millennia. There must be something in us that longs for the challenge of the hero's journey. The curiosity and longing I have always had is one aspect of my life that connects me to others. What I thought was a weakness or an emptiness is actually a strength, a gift that guides me forward into life, discovery, meaning, and truth.

At the very beginning in Genesis, the expulsion of Adam and Eve from the Garden of Innocence and Ease might be seen as the beginning of their journey. It can also be seen as symbolic of the beginning of the journey of humankind from innocence to rebellion, from struggle to surrender, from childhood to maturity.

When I began looking at the Old Testament with the idea of finding evidence of the resurrection principle, it seemed to leap from every page. Perhaps that proves that we find what we are seeking, but my awareness of the resurrection principle in my life has changed my entire way of looking at tragedy, loss, heartache, failure, and chaos. The resurrection principle helps me see possibility and promise in what appears to be hopelessness and disaster, and it helps me to ask different questions.

- If God is at work in all things, attempting to bring about good, where is God at work in this situation?
- If God is love, where is love blocked in this situation?
- If God is about freedom, where are we bound by biases, prejudices, fear, and judgment?
- What is God asking of me in this situation?
- Is this a place where God wants to use my gifts, or does this situation belong to someone else?

Those questions are vastly different from the questions people generally ask when life knocks us flat, such as these:

- Why did this happen to me? Why this? Why now?
- Why didn't God stop this? Whose fault is this?
- If God is love, why did he let this happen?

There are many reasons throughout history and certainly in the biblical record to build an intellectual denial of both God's existence and God's love. Some who won't read the Old Testament or who have read it from a certain perspective believe the Old Testament is about the "bad" God and the New Testament is about the "good" God. Perception is important, and we find what we are seeking.

The beginning of a new relationship with God was established with a covenant between Abram of Haran and Yahweh during a journey to an unknown land. Jacob's transformation was initiated by a forced journey following his stealing his twin brother's birthright and blessing, and Joseph, the favorite son of Jacob, was thrust into his journey when his brothers threw him in a pit to die. The journeys of those imperfect, struggling, stumbling beings reveal again and again that the God who calls us to journey and pilgrimage is with us all the way.

> *Whether you turn to the right or to the left, your ears will hear a voice behind you saying, This is the way; walk in it.*
>
> Isaiah 30:21

"Covenant" is almost a strange word to those of us who are shaped in a culture of deals, contracts, and legal agreements. It is based and built on the concept of reciprocal love, and, when offered by Yahweh, it was an unbreakable promise because God cannot *not* love that which he has created. The covenant of God to Abraham offered much to Abraham—land, progeny, blessing, protection, and greatness.

This covenant between Abraham and God did, however, have a proviso. It depended not on God's faithfulness but on Abraham's. God's faithfulness is constant. Abraham wobbled.

Some of us want all the benefits of God's presence, protection, and action, but we want to be free agents, keeping the commandments we choose and blowing off the others. Some of us want the gifts and fruit of the Holy Spirit, but we want to keep the Holy Spirit on retainer, calling him in on a crisis, relating to him "as needed."

However, God's love is constant, unrelenting, patient, protective, and seeking. God's love is faithful, fervent, and fierce, and perhaps the reason we quake at the thought of God is that we know we are so prone to want to live outside the covenant. We know how frail and flawed we are, how often we break our promises to the mere mortals with whom we live and work, and we doubt we can keep faith with God.

One of my favorite stories of God's provision for the strength, courage, and resilience to move forward is from the life of Jacob, son of Isaac and Rebekah, twin brother of Esau. Jacob's pilgrimage began not as a happy adventure or a call to take a hero's journey but with his being forced to leave home. He had stolen his brother's birthright and blessing, and my guess is that his first days on the road might have been spent turning the event over and over in his mind. Perhaps he wished he could take it all back. Perhaps he was filled with shame, or maybe he was angry at the circumstances that set him up to be the family outcast, of the warmth of home and family love.

Because we know the outcome of the story, the situation doesn't seem so bad, but if you are in the throes of a broken relationship with the people who matter most to you, it is hard to imagine reconciliation. The truth is that some family rifts never heal. Some arguments among friends are never resolved, and some relationships cannot bear the strain of betrayal. When you are in the midst of it, each person is likely to be on the defensive, justifying his actions, rationalizing her words, and proving who is right and who is wrong. To make things more painful, family members take sides or may distance themselves from all parties.

I love to imagine Jacob's bedding down on the road with so many thoughts tumbling over and over in his mind, falling asleep with a rock for a pillow and probably wishing for the comforts of home. The God-who-never-leaves-you intervened, however, with a dramatic dream of a ladder of angels ascending and descending. I believe God was reassuring Jacob that the heavenly messengers were carrying the prayers of his heart to God and communicating God's presence to Jacob.

Fortunately, Jacob recognized the holiness of that dream and built an altar there. His words, "Surely the Lord was in this place, and I did not know it," are words of reassurance we can carry with us as we journey along unknown and perhaps troubled paths.

God's presence remained with Jacob. In another nighttime intervention, on the night before he was to meet Esau for the first time since he had betrayed and tricked his twin, God's messenger wrestled with Jacob. My imagination leads me to think that perhaps in this wrestling match, Jacob was wrestling with what he had done to his brother, and that the wound to the thigh was a reminder that while the two men would be reconciled, the realities of what Jacob had done would remain.

I have learned that practicing resurrection sometimes means that the effects of choices I have made may not ever go away and that I may have to live with those effects, but those wounds can become not only bearable but even useful in softening my heart toward others who also live with heavy consequences. Some of our wounds don't go away, but we can learn to live with them in another way. In fact, those wounds we thought we couldn't bear may create in us compassion and empathy for others. Some of our wounds can make us what Henri Nouwen calls *wounded healers*.

> *Take the first step in faith. You don't have to see the whole staircase. Just take the first step.*
>
> ——Martin Luther King, Jr.

I can imagine the anxiety or fear with which Jacob rose the next morning to go out to meet his brother. I can imagine that he might have rehearsed what he would say and maybe what he would do, but it is clear that what happened between them and whatever choices they made, they experienced God's mercy in their reconciliation.

We often doubt that God really is the God of unconditional love, and we are hesitant to trust the Unseen because we have seen so much unfaithfulness, cruelty, and disrespect in ourselves and other human beings. Fortunately, God knows our weakness and has given us the presence of his love and power through the Holy Spirit, the Living Christ, to heal us, transform us, empower us, and liberate us.

Formed in a culture that teaches us to compete and defeat, to win at all costs, we understand contracts. It takes a leap of faith to understand *covenant*. "It's just a business deal," a man explained to me about the marriage of a young man and woman, and I felt chills of disbelief and resistance. I have a lifetime of belief in marriage as a sacred covenant that two people make out of love for each other. I grew up hearing my father's words to couples he married: "May your love for each other grow so that your chief joy is in giving happiness to the other." Marriage as a business deal didn't fit anything in my inner reference books or dictionaries. I only knew marriage as a partnership formed in love.

It is God's presence in the dark nights of the journey, in the twists and turns precipitated by wavering faith, bad choices, and even the lies we tell along the way, that is the power of new life and perseverance within us. It is God-at-work in our mistakes who transforms us in spite of our stupidities and impatience and outright defiance, sometimes working even in the messes we have made to reveal his love and his purpose.

God's presence with us empowers us to keep moving forward, to keep choosing life and love. God's presence is the resurrection principle within us, activating our hope, inspiring our courage, and generating the will to start over and work with him for good.

Of course, I cannot prove the existence of God, and the truth is that I write from the experience of having sensed both the presence and absence of God personally.

My challenge is not to convince anyone of the presence, action, or unconditional love of God but to write in such a way that I give true witness to what I have seen and heard and experienced, and what I have been told or have observed in others. It is that experience with God that charges my life with energy and purpose and meaning, and I simply give words as witness to that reality.

"The problem is that you aren't moving enough. You sit too much," my chiropractor told me.

I knew that what he said was true and that if I didn't listen to him, the results of a couple of falls and my extended time in front of my computer were going to get worse. At the time I first began working with this healer, I was in so much pain that I would have done anything he suggested. What I was not prepared for was how simple his suggestions would be or how long it would take for me to recover, going at the slow pace he recommended.

"Bodies are meant to move," he said. "You're going to have to get up and move around if you want to feel better."

The next day I read that "sitting is the new smoking," and I was living proof of the dangers and results of sitting too long at my computer, not taking breaks, not exercising.

It didn't take me long to connect the dots between this need for physical movement and the need for spiritual movement. Faith, after all, is active.

I do practice Centering Prayer, and I teach workshops on this powerful practice that asks for two twenty-minute "sits" each day. To be that still for that long requires great patience and stamina. It is an act of faith to believe that God is going to meet you in that time of waiting on him, and the truth is that the practice of sitting needs to be balanced with the practice of movement—acts of mercy and help, acts of generosity, participation, and compassion.

Both sitting and moving are acts of faith, and one without the other is incomplete.

Perhaps we are meant for spiritual movement—pilgrimage and journey—just as our physical bodies are meant to move, and the assurance we have is of God's presence with us. "Your teacher will be right there, local and on the job, urging you on whenever you wander left or right: 'This is the right road. Walk down this road'" (Isa 30:21, *The Message*).

Faith is a noun, but, even more, it is a verb. Hope is both the catalyst that moves us forward and the result of our actions.

Faith is about partnering with God or dancing with God, but it is movement with God, and here is the irony: when I am sitting still in the silence in my Centering Prayer practice, I am acting on the belief—the faith and the hope—that God is present and active within my life.

Faith becomes something you "have" only as you live it.

Faith is what gets us on the road of life and the journey; hope is what keeps us there.

Faith-hope-love all work together; they are not quite synonyms, but almost.

God is always at work, always bombarding us with his love, always reaching out.

Faith is the reason God is able to work with us, just as he worked with Abraham and Jacob.

We don't pray to be zapped by faith so that we can take action. We walk with whatever amount of faith we can muster, and the walk is our affirmation of faith.

God works in spite of our mistakes, with our mistakes, and perhaps because of them.

God is at work in situations that try us and test us, sometimes to our breaking points.

God intervenes as we are open to him, and sometimes even if we are not.

Questions to Ponder

1. What is the difference between a trip or sightseeing and a pilgrimage? What is the value of each?

2. From your point of view, do you see your life as a pilgrimage, a journey, a spectator sport, or a race to the finish line? Is this what you want, or do you want something different for yourself?

3. A project, meeting a health or financial crisis, a marriage, or parenting can be seen as a pilgrimage. Among those, which has turned out to be the most meaningful pilgrimage for you?

4. What kind of pilgrimage might be calling to you now?

5. How is growing in self-knowledge and authenticity a kind of pilgrimage?

I get the idea that I'm not in a
"put your little foot in" and
"take your little foot out" kind of
            experience this time.
   I can't get by with sticking
   my toe in the water now,
   and I don't think I'm going to
   get to test the temperature of
   the water.
It's sobering, really — it's really for real.
Once I take the first step,
            that's it.
"Don't turn back," he warned me,
his eyes blazing in the light of a
full moon.
      Dive in. Go for it.
      Trust the rapids of change.
Swim deep.
This is your life, you know.
      Take the plunge.
You'll never know how strong
you are until you surrender to the
path that has your name all over it.

Chapter 7

EASY IN THE HARNESS

How did I get myself in this mess?

I didn't see this coming! What am I going to do now?

What was I *thinking*?

Will this last forever?

Is there any way out?

Past the age of thirty, is there any one of us who hasn't experienced the pressure of feeling trapped or stuck in a situation from which we cannot seem to escape? Who doesn't know the flood of feelings when you realize that you have gotten in over your head or that the only way out of a hard situation is through it? Who doesn't know what it is like to take on a project, a job, or a relationship only to discover that the tasks before you are beyond your current abilities?

There is perhaps nothing more frustrating than feeling backed into a corner, stuck in a rut, and unable to see your way clear or see a way out.

"I feel as if I am just going around in circles, accomplishing nothing and getting nowhere," a friend told me, and I understood that feeling.

"This is for the rest of my life," an anguished person said. "I've got to deal with this every day from now on. There is no exit and I don't know that I can do it."

Most of our problems in life are solvable or at least endurable, especially if they are short-term or mere irritants or annoyances.

However, there are long-lasting issues, challenges, and tragedies, the effects of which are felt in all aspects of one's life.

There are burdens that we bear for ourselves and burdens we bear for others, so how do we find hope and strength that is beyond whatever natural resilience we might have? How do we learn to bear our long-term challenges with grace, authenticity, honesty, and courage?

It is for freedom that Christ has set us free. Stand firm, then, and so not let yourselves be burdened again by the yoke of slavery.

Galatians 5:1

"I'll never not be an addict," various people have told me through the years. "It's something I'm going to have to deal with every day of my life. I'm just one slip away from being in recovery to being a user."

Thankfully, there are resources now for managing our burdens, and the good news is that those resources are so good that millions of people have learned to live with serenity and emotional or physical sobriety, courage, and wisdom in recovery.

"It is a great paradox," a vibrant and joyful recovering addict told me. "You'd think that my addiction is the worst thing that ever happened to me and that recovery is limiting, when the truth is that if it weren't for this defect, I wouldn't know the depth of God's mercy and grace, and if it weren't for my recovery program, I would still be in bondage."

My own codependency, people-pleasing, and tendency to put others on the throne of my life have kept me on my knees for years, but the good news is that being on my knees has led me to a freedom I wouldn't have had any other way. Facing my own self-chosen demigods, naming them what they are, and then turning over my whole heart, mind, and soul—as much as I am able—to the care of God liberates and empowers me.

If there is one consistent story line in the Old Testament, it is the story that shows the ongoing struggle of the Hebrew people to stay free from slavery and oppressive leaders. Over and over, the people got slack in their worship of Yahweh, broke the commandments and the covenant they had made with God, or openly rebelled against his teachings, all of which made them vulnerable to being taken over by cruel leaders or placed in bondage. Miserable and repentant, they would cry out to God to free them. Finally, God would intervene, and in his consistent patience and provision he would lead them yet again out of oppression and bondage and into freedom.

There is much suffering among the Hebrew people, but the good news is that within the Old Testament there is consistent evidence of God's resurrection principle at work as he patiently worked for their good, even when they blocked his purpose and his love by ignorance, naiveté, carelessness, or outright rebellion. Nowhere is God's redemptive work more dramatic than in the story of Moses and the exodus of the children of Israel from Egypt.

There is something in us that yearns to be free, as surely as a plant turns toward the light, and there is something in us that recognizes that when we are in bondage to an addiction, a dysfunctional relationship, or a pattern of self-sabotaging behaviors, we are meant for more than slavery. There is something in us that cries out to be free, and I believe that the very crying out for freedom is evidence that God is at work in us, waking us up to the realities of our lives and to the call to be free.

I believe that our yearning for freedom and wholeness is itself the resurrection principle at work in what Jesus called the kingdom within.

The story of Moses in the Old Testament is one of the best stories for children because it contains such drama and excitement, beginning with the placing of the newborn Moses in a basket in the river to protect him from the dangers of being one of the Hebrew babies to be killed by order of the pharaoh. Children of all ages love the story of the burning bush, the drama of the plagues inflicted on the Egyptians, and the parting of the Red Sea, a miracle that was only the beginning of the arduous, difficult, and lengthy quest for freedom of the children of Israel.

As I read the story of Moses and the children of Israel, it is clear that God heard the cries of the enslaved Hebrews, but I wonder if the cry of Moses' heart might have been to be relieved of his guilt and regret over his murder of the Egyptian taskmaster. Left in the bondage of slavery to the Egyptians and, for Moses, the slavery of his past, the people could have either died in slavery or, with God's power, been delivered from slavery and set free to live in freedom.

Is it too much to suggest that the resurrection principle both activated their desire to be free and initiated the process of setting them free? With God's intervention, both Moses and the people moved from darkness into light, from bondage into freedom, from death of the spirit into resurrection.

If you hold to my teachings, you are really my disciples. Then you will know the truth, and the truth will set you free.

John 8:31b-32

All of us who struggle with powers that are greater than we can handle on our own are familiar with how long it takes from the recognition of the problem to the surrendering of the problem and then to the uneasy serenity and peace of emotional or physical sobriety. If only deciding to leave or put aside the thing that keeps us bound were the whole story, but the truth is that those of us who are in a process of freeing ourselves from the forces that bind us can identify with the forty years of wandering in the wilderness.

The story of the deliverance of the Hebrew people from the Egyptian pharaoh's bondage has fascinated me all my life, but recently I have turned my attention more to the transformation that occurred in the life of Moses.

Indeed, the people of Israel who stood at the border between bondage and the promise of freedom were set free. Those who followed Moses out of Egypt and out of bondage were changed by their wandering and changed by the difficulty of the desert, including the lack of food and water. They were to discover over many years the truth of a sentiment I heard long ago, that men are slaves because "freedom is hard and slavery is easy."[1]

I have to wonder about those who stood at the boundary between freedom and slavery and turned back to making bricks and living in subservience to Pharaoh. Did they regret not overcoming their fears or the laziness that usurps the freedom to choose, or were they content to be slaves?

I wonder, as well, about the people who did follow Moses on dry land with the waters of the Red Sea on either side but still had no idea what God was accomplishing in them and for them. Did some travel along, even arriving at the desired destination, never realizing that God was at work doing something new? Did some realize they were making history together, while others sauntered along, worrying about when the next meal would appear and where they might sleep at nightfall?

Could anyone have imagined the long struggle to get to the promised land? Did they assume that as soon as they walked out of Egypt, with the Red Sea parting before them, the work of freedom was accomplished? How upsetting it must have been when they realized how hard the walk to freedom would be! Can you blame them for grumbling and complaining?

Perhaps the children of Israel were not so different from those of us who stay asleep at the wheel of our lives, never rising to the occasion of recognizing the sacredness of our own life journey and never claiming the God-inspired and God-given freedom that is our birthright.

Whatever happened to the children of Israel as they left Egypt and journeyed together toward the promised land, we can learn a lot about the process of transformation by observing the work of God within the life of Moses.

The words that jump off the pages of my Bible reveal a deep, extraordinary, transforming intimacy between God and Moses. The way God intervened in the life of Moses to bring him out of the shepherd's pasture of his father-in-law and back to the site where he had murdered an Egyptian outside Pharaoh's palace, the place where this Hebrew child grew up in halls of power and privilege, speaks of the resurrection principle at work in a human instrument yielded to God.

Everything in Moses' history was preparation for his calling, but his hero's journey began as he left home, fleeing from the murder he had committed. Before Moses could take on the leadership of his people, he had to wander into his own wilderness, herding sheep for his father-in-law in a strange land. Perhaps even Moses had to be freed from his bondage of guilt and regret for having killed another man.

My imagination tells me that in those first years away from the comforts of Pharaoh's palace and away from any possible contact with his birth family, Moses' preparation happened within his spirit, where he may have wrestled with what he had done. My guess is that he suffered guilt and regret in those years, but might it not also be possible that what he had learned from his mother about his people and their relationship with Yahweh played over and over in his mind during the quiet days he spent in the pastures of his father-in-law?

Perhaps Moses remembered the stories he had heard about Abraham, Isaac, Jacob, and Joseph. Perhaps, as he tended sheep, he remembered the covenant relationship that God had initiated with his ancestors, and maybe it was pondering all of that and wondering about this Yahweh/God who walked and talked with his forbears that prepared the way for him to be awakened by the sight of the bush that was burning but not consumed.

You have freedom when you're easy in your harness.

—Robert Frost

Perhaps his longing for home and his people and his longing for Yahweh made Moses sensitive to the voice of God calling him to participate in a grand adventure. Surely, the proposition of setting his people free was a hero's journey, and it was appropriate for him to tremble with fear before the challenge of God's call.

Sometimes we are transformed and liberated by the actions of others, and sometimes we are transformed and liberated when we help others to freedom.

"I will tell you my story and walk with you to help you," my friend and Twelve Step sponsor told me repeatedly. "I want you to know, however, that there is a selfish reason I will do this, and it is that if I am going to stay free and sober, I must participate with others in their process. That is why we place so much importance on taking the Twelfth Step. We believe that we keep our freedom by telling another how it is that we have it."

As I read the story of Moses today, the part that teaches me the most is the intimate communication Moses maintained with God, even through the whining and complaining of the children of Israel and even though the process took so terribly long.

> *For to be free is not merely to cast off one's chains, but to live in a way that respects and enhances the freedom of others.*
>
> —Nelson Mandela

It was in those long years of walking and talking with God that Moses transformed from the man who quaked before the enormity of God's proposed task to a magnificent and strong leader. It was in his constant and consistent obedience to God and his unwavering faith that God was able to activate the resurrection principle in him and then use that transformation to inspire and lead his willful, rebellious flock.

If any hymn reveals Moses' faith, I think it is the one I heard my mother and grandmother sing so often, the old song "Trust and Obey." And if any memory verse describes Moses' active and steady faith, it is this: "Trust in the LORD with all your heart and lean not into your own understanding. In all your ways, acknowledge him, and he will direct your path" (Prov 3:5-6).

Leaning into my own understanding—trusting myself more than I do God or others, doing the same thing I've done over and over (whether it works or not), thinking I can outsmart the problem—gets me in trouble and actually prevents me from putting my trust in God, who is unseen, invisible, and therefore not instantly known.

How many times have I blasted forth with my own plan, only to find it as frustrating as the last plan I tried to do on my own? And how many times have I, like the children of Israel, lamented that God has surely abandoned me? Clearly, I enslave myself by my own self-will. I tie myself up in chains of my own making when my highly prized self-reliance runs wild and begins to work against me.

In my life, I have had to learn some hard lessons about freedom *from* the things that bind me and freedom *for* the abundant life that Christ promised and John records in John 10:10.

I have learned that some of the things to which I have been enslaved look good and maybe even are good. They certainly don't appear to be harmful, but they may not be what is right for me.

In doing spiritual direction with other people, I have become sensitive to watching for the ways others are bound and have learned that we are meant to be free from the things that keep us from becoming who we are intended to be.

We are to be free from what prevents us from fulfilling the purpose for which we were made.

We are to be free from the things I call our lesser gods or demigods, our addictions and our dependencies, whether those things are people, substances, or habits.

We are to be free from the intimidation of others over us and from anything that harms our bodies, souls, or minds, including a religious system that is oppressive in any of the various ways human beings concoct to keep others out of the circle of grace.

We are to be free from the lies we tell ourselves and the lies other people tell us about ourselves, even when those lies are wrapped in religious terminology—and maybe especially when those lies are religious lies.

We are to be free from our misunderstandings and wrong ideas about who God is, who we are to God, and what our relationship to God and the world is to be, and all of this liberation takes time and trouble, blood and sweat and tears.

Perhaps the arduous process of becoming free is part of what Paul meant when he said we are to work out our salvation with fear and trembling (Phil 2:12). Sometimes working out our salvation is doing what the children of Israel did, taking it one step at a time, but hopefully in the direction toward freedom.

The struggle to be free seems common to all humans, regardless of the time or place in which we live. We struggle to earn our freedom and then we struggle to maintain it, and sometimes we are asked to leave our comfort zones and participate in the emancipation and liberation of others.

When we are able to enter into another's suffering, holding out the light of hope and possibility, the freedom of Christ, and the promise of redemption in practical ways, we are participating with God in the work of the resurrection principle. In being Christ to each other, we are called and equipped to encourage and help others toward their own resurrection and transformation.

It is difficult to free fools from the chains they revere.

—Voltaire

It may be a long walk to freedom for any of us, and for some it's a longer walk than for others, but the process of taking the walk together is itself healing, transforming, liberating, and empowering.

❧ ❧ ❧

In all recovery programs (and truly, in all of life), it is important to take periodic inventories of your personal life. Dr. James Hollis, Jungian analyst and author, often said that it is a good idea to take a personal inventory about every seven years to see what is still working for you, what you need to change or discard in your daily life, and what adjustments you need to make.

Use the following lists to assess the quality of your personal freedom. This exercise deserves and requires time and reflection. Don't try to rush through it; instead, take time to listen to the truth that dwells within you. Dare to be boldly honest.

Instead of overwhelming yourself with too many inner projects at once, choose one or two to face, work with, and give up. Then you can move to another one.

We are to be free from . . .

. . . the things that keep us from being and becoming who we are intended to be.

. . . the things that have become our lesser gods, our idols, our addictions.

. . . the intimidation of others over us.

. . . that which harms our bodies, minds, or souls.

. . . that which prevents us from fulfilling our purpose in life.

. . . the lies we believe.

. . . a wrong or harmful God-image that is inconsistent with the biblical image of Christ.

. . . a wrong understanding of who we are and our place in the world.

. . . our need to control, have power over, or imprison others.

. . . depression.

. . . oppression.

. . . fear, guilt, and shame, anger or hate, insecurities.

Questions to Ponder

Take some time to ponder the habits, substances, mindsets, people, and other things that bind you. Ask yourself questions like these:

- How big is this problem in my life?
- How did it start? What purpose has it served?
- What have I missed from wearing this chain?
- What could I gain by surrendering this chain to God and allowing him to free me?
- What is stopping me from letting go, making changes, letting freedom win?

We are to be free for . . .
. . . the abundant life.
. . . living into our full nature of being made in the image of God.
. . . becoming the True Self God created us to be.
. . . being spontaneous, living in the present moment.
. . . being comfortable and at home in our own skin.
. . . giving generously and freely of our resources to others.
. . . allowing the Spirit of God to flow freely through us, producing the fruit of the Spirit.
. . . living our own unique purpose in life.
. . . enjoying pleasure, delight, and joy in daily life.

Take some time to ponder the freedoms to which you are entitled. Assess what is lacking in your life and what is flowing freely in your life. Ask yourself questions like these:

• What do I want most from this list?
• Do I believe God intends for me to have all of these freedoms?
• What can I do to "help God help me" access and appropriate the freedoms for which I am made?

Note

1. This may have been an adaptation of an idea expressed in the Latin phrase, "*Malo periculosam, libertatem quam quietam servitutem*," translated variously as "I prefer the tumult of freedom over the quiet of servitude" or "I prefer dangerous freedom over peaceful slavery." Both Thomas Jefferson and Jean Jacques Rousseau used this phrase in their writing.

If I'm going to make this pilgrimage . . .
If I'm going to take this walk to freedom . . .
If I'm going to follow you, Loving God . . .
keep my heart calm
make my mind clear
make my steps sure
keep me steady on the path

If I'm going to make this journey . . .
help me take myself lightly
stop me when I think too hard
and help me walk more and analyze less.
Keep me, please, O Gracious God,
from judging how I'm doing
criticizing the rocks in the path
Give me, please, the grace I need
to keep walking forward.

If I'm going to walk this path
If I'm going to choose this way
If I'm going to ask and knock and seek
Please give me the stamina and courage I need,
but more,
Give me the willingness to let you lead . . . lead me home.

Chapter 8

MINING FOR GOLD

"With everything in me, I wish I could turn back the clock and have a redo. What I did was wrong, and I have hurt so many people."

I have heard similar words many times from people who are courageous enough to speak the truth, take responsibility for their actions, and be humble enough to accept the forgiveness of God and move forward.

As a spiritual director, I sit in the silence and offer my presence as an instrument of God's great love. I know that when a person has the courage to admit his or her wrong to another person, it is a holy moment. It is not my job to censure or condemn; generally, people have enough self-condemnation to last a lifetime. My job is to look for what God is attempting to do in the directee's life to bring peace and joy into the brokenness.

"Why can't I move on from this failure? What keeps me circling back to the same thing, punishing myself one more time? If I could just believe God has forgiven me, I could move on!"

Often, the phrase *move on* feels so permanent, as if you are cutting yourself off from the past. The words "moving on" are often said with impatience or judgment either to ourselves or by others who are tired of rehashing the same old problem. Moving on indicates escaping and moving away from that which is painful or hard, but the truth is we will carry some things forever as consequences of choices we have made, often in a twenty-second lapse of judgment. Can any one of us really shut and forever lock the door of the past?

"I have run away from my pain for my entire life, moving from one job to another, one girlfriend to another, trying to run from myself. The only problem is that wherever I go, I take myself with me!"

Does the fact that we carry our past and the consequences of our choices mean God has not forgiven us or is not willing to forgive us? Clearly not.

Is it possible to carry those consequences in a new, redemptive way? Yes indeed!

Perhaps a simple change of wording from moving on to *moving forward* may be semantics, but it feels more hopeful. Moving on implies a cutoff from the past, an estrangement that is still with us, draining energy from us like all unacknowledged pain does.

Without exception, that change in wording to *moving forward* has had a positive effect on the people to whom I have suggested it. Even if a person has been wallowing in a past grievance or wrong, to insist that she *move on* sets up resistance and often a sigh and perhaps tears. "I know I should move on, but . . ." is often the response.

Moving forward somehow communicates a pace that is doable, patience with oneself, as if it is okay to move unsteadily, even hesitantly, but forward.

When it is time, I introduce the concept of *practicing resurrection*, offering it as a spiritual practice, a choice, a conscious decision to work with God in shaping a grace-filled present and future.

"What does *practicing resurrection* mean for me?" someone asked in the yearlong study I taught for my Thursday Morning Bible Study. I took the question as a challenge.

"I can't find my way," the woman said, "but when you use that term, I want to know how to do that."

If you read the history of the children of Israel, you see the constant presence of God, offering forgiveness, mercy, love, and compassion. In the biggest messes we can make, there is God, attempting to bring about good. Practicing resurrection calls for a change of mind, a more focused spiritual practice, talking it over with someone who is on the side of hope for you. It calls for a decision to work within *what is*

Oh these foolish men. They could not create so much as a worm, but they create gods by the dozens.

—Michel de Montaigne

instead of denying it, avoiding it, repressing it, or suppressing it. We learn to acknowledge, admit, accept, and process.

Consciously choosing resurrection as a spiritual practice can change your life. I have proven the possibility to myself, moving forward out of a season of sadness and grief and intentionally choosing radical hope as a gift from God day by day. It takes effort and consciousness to change my mind, and my heart sometimes lags behind, but the internal change works to effect outer change.

"It was the worst time in my life. I wish what happened had never happened, but it did. I have to live with it forever, and sometimes it is too much for me."

Life happens to all of us eventually, and we have varying degrees of faithfulness to God, despite our repeated vows to be faithful and consistent.

Grace and mercy make it possible for people to move from a feeling of desperation and despair over the past to a place of being able to say, "I wish it hadn't happened. It was the worst thing in my life, but somehow, over time and with a lot of help from stand-ins for God, it was also the best thing that could have happened to me."

Even if they cannot say it was the best thing, people who have worked through a problem to grace can nearly always say, "I learned something important from the experience."

I have heard those words many times and have watched many people rise from the ashes of disappointment and despair; it is another practice that echoes Paul's words when he says in Philippians 2:12,

"Continue to work out your salvation with fear and trembling . . . ."
Don't miss what follows in verse 13: ". . . for it is God who works in
you to will and to act according to his good purpose."

God working in you for good is the definition of practicing
resurrection!

I am particularly fond of the way Eugene Peterson says this great
truth in *The Message*:

> Better yet, redouble your efforts.
> Be energetic in your life of salvation, reverent and sensitive before
> God.
> That energy is God's energy, an energy deep within you,
> God himself willing and working at what will give him the most
> pleasure.

Sometimes, amazingly, we prefer to stay in the pit or are afraid
to rise from it out of fear that maybe the pit is more real than the
possibility of hope.

One of the amazing and wonderful things about the Bible is that
nothing is hidden. Our heroes are shown with their flaws, their sins,
and their suffering, and with the gift of knowing their failures, we
find wisdom for our own struggles to keep hope alive in our hearts. It
is perhaps cold comfort to suggest that there is a potential gift within
our failures, a blessing to be uncovered in our setbacks, or something
good in the worst thing that happens to us.

Let me be clear that when someone is in the midst of the shock of
a loss or is bearing the pain of sorrow, that is not the time to present
the idea that something good can come out of heartbreak. Good
news in the bad news must be saved for later, and it is best discovered
by the person bearing the heartbreak and not forced by some cheerful
optimist who needs to spread cheer to make himself feel better.

There is no way to express the comfort and hope I felt when someone said to me, "You will get through this, and I will be with you while you travel this path."

Mercy and grace rushed into my experience when a wise helper said to me, "As long as it takes, I will listen to you, but I know that your grief will lose its hard edges, with time and God's faithfulness." Because he believed, I leaned on his faith and learned to believe. I appreciate the gift of a quiet and steady presence of a friend who understands the process of redemption and knows that resurrection in daily life will take as long as it takes.

You shall have no other gods before me. You shall not make for yourself an idol.

Exodus 20:3-4

"If I could just understand why this happened and why it happened to me! If only I could find the reason, I think I would feel better."

Sometimes, it is possible for us to know why some of the bad things happen to good people we know, but sometimes "the reason" is hidden from us. In fact, some tragedies defy human logic or understanding. Some sorrows seemingly come upon us from out of the blue, and continuing to demand an answer to the "why" questions means remaining in constant turmoil or fascination.

The "why" questions lead us around in circles, and even if you know what caused a particular tragedy, continuing to ask "Why me?" "Why now?" and "Why this?" leads only to dead ends and misery.

I've thought about these mysteries of tragedy and trial for most of my life. As a minister's daughter, I was introduced to hard suffering early in my childhood. Because my parents were there when tragedies occurred in the lives of our congregation, I often heard about them (though my parents did try to shield me from death and suffering). Now a minister's wife, I better understand that pastors often exist in the midst of raw suffering with the people for whom they are shepherd, and pastors' families often bear witness to that pain. In my own life I have had to face nocturnal wanderings, wrestling with my unanswered questions and with God, who remained supremely silent, sometimes invoking my deepest sorrow.

I have written about suffering in my book on Job, but what I see in the entire Old Testament only serves to reinforce a lifelong belief that God draws near to us when we are suffering. While his absence often seems more real than his presence, if we can tolerate Job's ash heap long enough and endure the interrogations or explanations of our so-called friends who want to make themselves feel better, somehow we can come to a place where the wrestling stops and we can accept the peace and comfort of the Living God.

My affirmation of faith is that God is available to us when we are in the deepest, darkest pit of despair, if only we can cry out for him. It is not, however, that we cry out loudly enough to finally get God's attention. It is because it is the nature and character of God to hear our cries.

I rely on these words in Psalm 34:18: "The LORD is close to the brokenhearted and saves those who are crushed in spirit."

And these words in Psalm 147:3 are underlined and dated often in my Bible: "The LORD heals the brokenhearted and binds up their wounds."

I can witness to the truth in these verses, not because they are in the Bible but because I have experienced the work and action of God in my own dark nights of wrestling and fear.

We humans fail, and sometimes we fail miserably. We repeatedly fall short of the glory of God. We are recalcitrant, and yet we often long to be better people, more faithful people, steadier and more consistent people.

Whatever any of us has done, however, we can rest in the prickly assurance that we aren't the first and we won't be the last to suffer at the hands of others, struggle with our own wrong actions, and carry loads of guilt, pain, anguish, regret, and shame. It's part of the hard stuff of being human.

For me, it is now a spiritual practice to look for the meaning in a situation instead of asking the "why" questions. It is far more helpful in moving forward to ask, "What does this mean for me now?" and to be alert to see where and how and in what ways God works to bring meaning to me in the fullness of time.

Further, I may be able to face some of the hard reasons something has happened, and they may be reasons that break my heart even more. I may be able to see what someone did or did not do that caused a tragedy, either out of willful intent, carelessness, or rebellion, but even in that, asking "why?" somehow adds to the pain.

Asking "Where is God at work in this?" opens my mind to accept the presence of God in the midst of sorrow. Asking "Why didn't God stop this?" leads me only to despair.

"I cannot believe I did that! I know better. I did the very thing I said I would never do, and I have neglected to do the things I set out to do!"

Quoted in Romans 7:18-29, the Apostle Paul said, "For I have the desire to do what is good, but I cannot carry it out. What I do is not what I want to do; no, the evil I do not want to do, I keep on doing."

Paul may have said it, but I have heard those words out of the anguish of more human beings than I can count. Indeed, we have a hard time reconciling our failures and imperfections, but the sooner we can admit that we are capable of doing whatever any other human is capable of doing, the more quickly we can face our capacity for harm and make corrections.

When we can admit that had we been born into the same circumstances as the most dangerous criminal, we might have done what they did, we can then accept our humanity. We accept our humanity when we can look at the person we deplore and say, "There but for the grace of God go I."

The Bible offers so much help if we will look for it as wisdom, grace, and mercy. Approaching the biblical narrative as a love story filled with forgiveness leads to a far different relationship with Scripture than looking for the rules and the corresponding punishments that are guaranteed if you don't follow the rules, especially those that were made in ancient times for primitive and nomadic people.

The story of the children of Israel is the story of a cycle repeated over and over. Out of slavery in Egypt and equipped with the Ten Commandments to help them live in new freedom with Yahweh and with each other, they entered the promised land. If only they had followed the Ten Commandments and stayed close to God, everything might have been different.

Given the burden and blessing of the power to choose, however, they drifted away from God, made up their own rules and laws, and lived as if they knew better than Yahweh how to live. Over and over in a sad cycle, they wandered away from God, either by carelessness, neglect, ignorance, or outright rebellion, and found themselves under bondage to yet another ruler. Maybe they took their chosen-ness to mean something other than God intended it to mean.

> *Men rarely (if ever) invent gods superior to themselves. Most gods have the morals and manners of a spoiled child.*
>
> —Robert Heinlein

The history of the Israelites that is recorded in the Old Testament includes those terrible cycles of bondage, but it also includes the constant and relentless pursuit of his people by God.

Indeed, the Bible is filled with warfare, oppression, violence, and suffering, but with eyes finely tuned to the love of God, you will see that love in abundance.

If you read the Old Testament stories with a sensitivity to the work of God in the midst of the peoples' lives, what you see throughout their history is the plaintive and consistent plea of God, calling out to his people, "Return to me. Come back to me!"

The clarion call of the Source of unconditional love is constantly reaching out to his people, patiently pursuing them, longing for their return, and providing specific people to sound that call of love to bring them back. We know those people as the prophets in the Old Testament.

Through all of the history of the Hebrew people, we see God, the Lover of all, extending his mercy and compassion, help and healing to his people, his beloved ones.

Contained within the message of each of the prophets of the Old Testament are instructions and correctives for the people, and, seen from the perspective of God, the Lover, aren't they messages of reconciliation and restoration? Isn't God's constant wooing of the people evidence of his love, and isn't his beckoning to them to return to him a sign of hope, a recognition that there is no place we can go that is outside the scope of God's love?

To look at the Hebrew people and their relationship with God is to look at our own lives and gain wisdom from them. It is not helpful to look at the Old Testament stories and interpret them such that God is a mean and vengeful God.

Here is what the Old Testament prophets did say to the children of Israel:

- You have broken God's laws.
- You have strayed away from God and your devotion to him.
- You defy God by your actions and your words.
- You have begun abusing people for your own use or depriving them of basic needs.
- You have become arrogant, seeking power over others.
- You have neglected to care for widows, orphans, and those who cannot care for themselves.
- You dare to offer fancy worship to try to make God forget. (See Isa 1:13.)
- And because you keep on doing this, you will reap the crop you have planted.

It is unbearably hard to sit and listen to someone tell us a painful and difficult truth about ourselves, to face us with our wrongdoing and be the messengers of the cold, hard facts we want to avoid. It is humiliating to fall from grace in our own eyes and, like Job, be exposed for what we have done that we long to hide, and yet there is good news in finally having the hard, ugly, and embarrassing facts out in the open.

Stripped of our pride, laid bare before God, naked and ashamed, we find ourselves able to rise from the ashes and move toward resurrection.

The Old Testament prophets called out to the people, a sign that God had not given up on them. Likewise, our ability to cry out to God indicates, I believe, that we have not given up on God. God's words of conviction from the mouths of the prophets opened the door for new life for the recalcitrant, stiff-necked, hard-hearted, and hard-headed ancestors in the faith from whom we can learn much.

What can we glean from these long-ago events that have meaning for our lives when we are in the pit of despair, sitting on Job's ash heap of abject suffering or wallowing around in an agitation of self-blame, self-recrimination, and self-flagellation?

How can we grasp at the slender thread of resurrection hope and put ourselves in a position that makes it possible for God to help us?

I will never forget the moment when I came to the age of account-ability, and it was long past the time when I had accepted Christ as my personal savior.

Sitting in the office of the Jungian analyst with whom I did my depth analysis, I was pushing back against something he said to me about being responsible for an incident that had happened years before. I can't remember exactly what it was, but the details do not matter. What matters is what I was about to learn.

"I'm not responsible for that," I began, hoping to explain to him that what we were discussing had *happened* to me. It wasn't my fault, in other words. We were discussing a hardship inflicted on me, a wrong done to me, and I was invested in keeping the blame and fault with the other person.

"You are responsible for that," he said firmly.

I didn't much like him in that moment.

"You may not have caused it," he went on. "It may have been done to you, but if you will take responsibility for how you are carrying it now, it can transform you."

My mind went through a few revolutions, trying to figure out how I could continue to shift the blame onto the right parties. He let me sit and stew for a few moments, and then he spoke words of grace.

"All of that happened. It's in the past. What will you do now? You and only you can be responsible, for you can decide if you are going to let that define you."

So many times, I had cried out David's prayer to God: "My God! Rescue me from my enemies, defend me from these mutineers. Rescue me from their dirty tricks, save me from their hit men" (Ps 59:1-2).

My self-punishment was blaming myself for what others had done, telling myself that if I had been more acceptable, smarter, better, holier, or more adequate, I wouldn't have deserved the wounds they had inflicted on me. If only I had done a better job, or if only I had been *enough*, I could have prevented so many things.

I didn't like having to face up to the ways I was living in a victim's stance, a stance that had always repelled me in others. In that sacred analytic container, confronted by the truth of my life, I finally felt safe enough to understand and then accept that if I was ever going to be free, I needed to shake off, somehow, the chains of the inner pharaohs, tyrants, and taskmasters and give up the self-defeating habits of a lifetime.

Frankly, those habits had become my security blankets, and I was scared to change my mind, change my ways, and change my life.

Here's the hard and good news about trouble and trauma, pain and suffering: no matter what lies at the root of your discomfort or distress, when you are able to see that within that *thing*—that event, that crisis, that loss, that tragedy—God is at work to bring about good. The very thing you want to avoid, deny, or run from may contain what God wants to use to heal you, transform you, liberate you, and empower you to live the life you are created to live.

There is no Old Testament figure who lost or suffered more than poor Job, but his long sit on the ash heap, wrestling with his old understanding of who God was, an understanding that he could never recover, cracked open his mind and heart so that he could finally understand God wanted not his purity or his perfect life, his perfect family or his perfect righteousness, but his heart. On that ash heap of suffering, God was at work in Job's innermost being, below the ego's control and beneath his consciousness, transforming a broken, humiliated, wounded man's whole religious structure and showing him that the Redeemer is not a taskmaster to be placated but the Beloved to be loved.

Trauma and heartache can dismantle our defenses so that we become open to the power of repentance. Pain can soften us so that we are not as resistant to the guidance that comes from God through a person, a seemingly casual comment, or a directional sign that appears out of nowhere and may mean nothing to anyone but us.

A framed quote sits over my desk, and it reminds me of my pattern. "I walk. I stumble. I fall. I get up . . . and I start over."

How are we to know the difference between the voices who are real helpers, healers, and prophets and those who sing a siren song that only serves to sink us deeper into the pit or transfer us to another pit?

How do we know that what has come across our path is there merely to rescue us and not deliver us? How do we avoid escaping into denial or avoidance? What if we just want to feel better and not really have to change?

In 1 John 4:1 the writer says, "Dear friends, do not believe every spirit, but test the spirits to see whether they are from God, because many false prophets have gone out into the world." How do we do that when we need guidance, direction, and help?

It can be hard to know who to follow, especially if the person before us is speaking religious language and seems to be speaking for God!

How do we move forward with discernment, especially when the process of resurrection and rebirth is tedious, laborious, and slow? If only we all could be transformed in the twinkling of an eye!

In my life, I've had wonderful teachers and mentors along the spiritual path. It's been important to me that the guides and companions whom I have chosen have an understanding of God that is, as far as I can tell, consistent with the biblical model.

I have also had people who acted as prophets in my life, speaking the truth to me about forces and tendencies that kept me stuck, telling the truth about what would happen to me if I continued down the path I was on.

Those who have been willing to speak the truth to me have shared it with the authority of love. I have known the power of hard and confrontational words coming from people who had earned their right to speak to me honestly and boldly.

You shall love the Lord your God with all your heart, mind and soul, and your neighbor as yourself.

Matthew 22:37-39

Taking the life of Job as a model, it is important for me to own my responsibility for what I have done, but it is not helpful or right for me to take on the responsibility that belongs to others. It is not being critical to admit what others have done, and in fact, sobriety and sanity often depend on a person's taking some of the blame off his shoulders and allowing another to carry his rightful share of it.

Job refused to be lured back into his old religious system that said that his troubles were the result of a sin he had not confessed. Refusing to be pressured by his so-called friends about his hideous plight, Job stayed silent and let God work on his inner life.

Sometimes now, years after I took my first journey through the Twelve Steps in an attempt to recover from codependency, I am astonished at how quickly I can regress into old patterns. I'm also grateful when I can regain my balance, return to Step One again, and get back on my program.

Thankfully, I've learned that relapses and regressions can be a necessary and important part of recovery, and I've learned that returning to the faith practices that build inner strength is a good thing. While the slip keeps me humble, it also keeps me in practice, returning to my knees and reminding me to be conscious that I am always standing in the need of prayer and help and aid—and that this is not only okay but also natural.

In the Seventh Step, we "humbly ask God to remove our shortcomings," and I think that "humbly" may be the key word in that step. We ask, knowing that this is not a "once and for all" prayer and that we will need to return to it. This step is, then, an ongoing practice, held with an awareness that acknowledges the reality that even as we strive to stay sober and serene, we humans remain forever and eternally imperfect and subject to falling back into old patterns.

The lyrics and music of Leonard Cohen are so full of mercy and grace, especially in "Anthem."

> Ah, the wars they will
> be fought again.
> The holy dove,
> She will be caught again
> bought and sold
> and bought again.
> The dove is never free.

Far from being discouraged that I must live with my imperfections and shortcomings, I find encouragement in Cohen's words. *I am not a failure because I struggle with my darker angels, my insecurities, my scars, and my wounds.* In fact, the very imperfections I carry can make me more compassionate to others, more connected to the human race, and kinder and more tenderhearted toward those who, like me, struggle toward redemption. I am never completely healed on this plane, and that keeps me on the journey; the journey keeps me alive and aware, discovering new horizons and exploring new possibilities.

So it is with this step that I have learned a powerful life lesson. In accepting myself as I am—good and bad, strong and weak, loving and unloving, generous and selfish, critical and merciful, unforgiving and forgiving, humble and proud—I can be at peace.

By contrast, in living within the hard and unyielding bars of either/or—perfect or imperfect, good or bad, worthy or worthless, wise or foolish, strong or weak—I am doomed to the prisons of my own making. I remind us again of Frederick Buechner, who reassures us in *The Final Beast* that our worst thing doesn't have to be our last thing, and that is pure grace to me:

> The worst isn't the last thing about the world. It's the next to the last thing. The last thing is the best. It's the power from on high that comes down into the world, that wells up from the rock-bottom worst of the world like a hidden spring. Can you believe it? The last, best thing is the laughing deep in the hearts of the saints, sometimes our hearts even. Yes. You are terribly loved and forgiven. Yes. You are healed. All is well.

Cohen sings about mercy and grace like this in the opening stanza of "Anthem":

> The birds they sang
> at the break of day
> Start again
> I heard them say
> Don't dwell on what has passed away
> or what is yet to be.
> Ring the bells that still can ring.
> Forget your perfect offering.
> There is a crack, a crack in everything.
> That's how the light gets in.

And I say *Amen.*

I love the idea that you can start the day over any time you need to, and I love the mercy in the slogan "one day at a time." I love knowing that sometimes you can take it an hour at a time or a breath at a time.

I've breathed my way through many hard moments, wavering between my failures and self-punishment, and reminding myself of this Scripture just before I slip into the familiar and seductive arms of my shortcomings that are always somewhere, lurking where I cannot see them:

> Because of the LORD's great love we are not consumed,
> for his compassions never fail.
> They are new every morning;
> great is your faithfulness. (Lam 3:22-23)

God's great love is the spark of the resurrection principle within us.

Questions to Ponder

1. What was the biggest mistake you ever made?

2. Have you ever fallen from grace in your own eyes?

3. When have you tried to wiggle out of taking responsibility for something you have done?

4. How have you experienced the grace (God's undeserved favor for you) or mercy (God's protection in the mess you have made) or justice (God's working to make things right)?

5. How has God used your imperfections to give you his love?

❦ ❦ ❦

I can't decide whether to square my shoulders, stand up straight
and bear the punishment I deserve
or
to fall on my face and ask what penance I can pay for what I've done
or
maybe I should fall to my knees and beg for mercy.

Somewhere, even in this mess, I hear a Voice that beckons to me.
Even now, I can see a Light that shines in this pit of darkness.
Even I . . . have not wandered so far away that I do not feel God's Love.

God of Mercy, God of Grace,
Am I calling out to You or are You calling out to me?
And how is it that even in this darkness
Your power and presence are real to me?
How is it that I can know You are here, now,
when I have wandered so far away, on my own,
striking out in defiance?

Redeemer, have you really come to buy me back . . .
or did You ever leave me?
Here, at this extremity . . . Here I am.
And so are You.

Chapter 9

I AM THE ONE

It's really hard when you have fallen from grace in your own eyes.

It's such a pain to have to lie in the bed you have made for yourself.

Looking into the eyes of someone you love, whom you have also hurt, is so painful and difficult that it is sometimes impossible for some people to do.

Don't we love to tell the stories about the young shepherd boy David, playing on his harp and composing the psalms that comfort and sustain us through the valleys of the shadows? Don't we love to ponder his rise from shepherd boy to the great king of Israel?

While touring Israel in 1992, I visited the area thought to be King David's tomb, and I was struck by the reverence of the other visitors to the site. When I look at David's seduction of Bathsheba and the way he covered his guilt by having her husband murdered, I struggle to reconcile the competing parts of his story.

I don't know why I should be surprised at the struggle of David because I, too, struggle with the competing parts of my inner motivations, actions, and feelings. I, too, am conscious of the broken places in my life and the ways I try to cover my tracks, pretend that what I did wasn't as bad as what my friend did, excuse myself and justify my ways.

It was in my adulthood that I got beyond the stories of the little shepherd boy David to the story of his adultery with Bathsheba, and then to his ordering that her husband be sent to the front lines of a battle. The part of the story that riveted my attention was the moment when prophet and chronicler of Hebrew history, Nathan, confronted King David with the truth about his sin. Friend and counselor to the great king, Nathan showed his true friendship by telling a story about a man who had done a similar thing, thus angering David. Then, the friend who dared to speak the truth to power spoke the famous words, "You are the man!"—thereby blowing David's cover of self-righteousness and forcing him to repentance and finally, to forgiveness (see 2 Samuel 11–12).

Fortunate is the person who has a friend true enough to say to you, "You are the one." Blessed is the person who is able to admit, "I am the one," for it is the ability to speak the hard truth to oneself and say, "I did this" that is the first step in healing. It is the strength to admit you have done wrong against God and another and yourself that sets in motion the blessed redemption of God.

I didn't hear these stories about the great psalm writer and king when I was a child, but there is perhaps no story that touches me more deeply in the Old Testament

For I have the desire to do what is good, but I cannot carry it out. For what I do is not the good I want to do; no, the evil I do not want to do—this I keep on doing. . . . What a wretched man I am.

Romans 7:18b-19

than the account of Nathan's confronting David with what he had done. I hold my breath as I read how skillfully Nathan led David to the truth by causing David to be angry against a man in a story. David's defensive reaction hid his guilt, but Nathan led David to an awakening that changed his life.

I stand in awe of the courage and honesty of Nathan when he looked David in the eye and said, "You are the man," which brought David to a stunning moment of seeing himself as he really was and then declaring, "I have sinned against the Lord."

If only all people could have a friend as loving as Nathan; if only all of us were able to bow before the truth and admit the truth about ourselves.

My story isn't the same as the story of King David's adultery, murder, and lies, but I know what it is like to face the darkness within me and call it what it is.

I know what it is like to want mercy for myself but justice for others.

Set against David's great sin are the beautiful words of repentance in Psalm 51 that are attributed to King David. Against the pain of my own sin, I pray those ancient words for myself, and with my prayer, I am led to the encounter with my darkness and the admission of my sin against God and others, and that honesty somehow opens the doorway for the mercy and forgiveness of God to flow into my life.

It is with relief and a sense of urgency that I return every year to the beginning of the Lenten season when, on Ash Wednesday, I repeat the words of David's penitent prayer, and those words are mine once again. With relief and trust I return to the season of Lent and a prayer from the Book of Common Prayers. God's resurrection principle draws me to confession; his work in me makes me yearn for the kneeling bench and the words of confession.

Most merciful God,
we confess that we have sinned against you
in thought, word, and deed,
by what we have done,
and by what we have left undone.
We have not loved you with our whole heart;
we have not loved our neighbors as ourselves.
We are truly sorry and we humbly repent.
For the sake of your Son Jesus Christ,
have mercy on us and forgive us;
that we may delight in your will,
and walk in your ways,
to the glory of your Name. Amen.
(The Book of Common Prayer, p. 360)

The refusal to admit a wrongdoing and confess it sets up a condition in which hope and trust in God die. Hope dies with our refusals to come clean before God, and those refusals set up a cycle of distrust and distance between people who should be able to live in the freedom of honesty and openness with each other.

To admit duplicity and deception to yourself is hard enough, but to have to look into the eyes of a friend, a parent or child, a spouse, or a colleague or supervisor and admit a wrong is a terrible challenge. To confess a crime is wrenching, and if you have lost the ability to do even that, then you add another layer of terribleness. That which we do not admit and own, talk about, and work out within ourselves, we are prone to project upon or take out on others.

For I know my transgressions, and my sin is always before me. Against you, you only, have I sinned and done what is evil in your sight.

Psalm 51:3-4

My life experience has taught me that without confession, repentance, and a desire not only to live another way but also to make amends for what I have done to injure either myself or others, hope begins to die. Unconfessed wrong festers, destroying the possibility of experiencing mercy and grace and setting up an endless cycle of repetitions of the same self-destructive behaviors. That which is not forgiven has an uncanny way of repeating itself. Getting by with the ways we humans fall from grace eventually does something terrible to our souls, not to mention to others who fall victim to our wrongdoing.

In my inner work, which involves nurturing my soul with prayer, meditation, spiritual reading, and self-analysis, I have learned the necessity of keeping the lines of communication open with the people I love. My commitment to this way of life, formed largely by working the Twelve Steps of Recovery, is helped by a willingness to own my character defects and be aware of how insecurity, inadequacy, shame, guilt, hate, anger, and fear—what I learned to call the Big Sins—cause me to commit the sins of action and word.

As long as I confess only the action I have done, I stand vulnerable to repeating it. If I can trace back to the afflictive emotion that caused the action, that is where real redemption happens. Confessing the action is like flailing away at the smoke; confessing the motivation of my heart gets to the fire that causes the smoke.

Admitting that anything another human might do, I also could do, given the same circumstances, timing, and opportunity, is humbling and often humiliating. Any self-examination, for the purpose of confession, is an opportunity to join the human race.

If I were running the world, which I most assuredly am not, I would reinstate the confession booth as a means to keeping hope alive because authentic hope is infused with the mercy and grace of God, available to all who are willing to receive it.

My friend Charlotte Sullivan asked if I had ever heard of Leonard Cohen, and when I told her I had not, she pressed a CD in my hand and said, "I think you will like his work." (I do understand that CDs are part of the last century. I get it that Sonos and Spotify are the way to go, but I'm still fond of my CDs.)

I took the CD home and popped it into my player, and when I first heard the voice of Leonard Cohen, I could not imagine why my friend had given me a copy of one of his CDs. That she had said, "I think you might like this," shocked me because she knew me well and was surely aware of my musical taste. I put the CD away, but thankfully I didn't give it away.

Hearing singer k.d. lang's stunning performance of

Like a bird on the wire, like a drunk in a midnight choir

I have tried in my way to be free . . .

Like a baby stillborn, like a beast with his horn,

I have torn everyone who reached out to me.

—"Bird on the Wire,"
Leonard Cohen

Cohen's now-classic "Hallelujah" at the opening of the 2010 Olympics in Vancouver led me to my cabinet to find the rejected CD. With new ears, I became a fan of both lang and Cohen.

Listening closely to the words of Cohen's music, I kept having the feeling that he was a mystic with a deep spirituality, but nothing out of the hymnals of my religious life matched his music. And yet I kept hearing biblical references, symbols from the Old and New Testament, and I got curious about his religious and spiritual tradition.

In a full-page, color article about Cohen's hometown of Montreal, Canada, in the *New York Times* on February 12, 2017, he is referred to as "the godfather of gloom" and "the poet laureate of pessimism."

I had to smile when I read those words because I could have said them myself when I first heard his voice, but after reading *I'm Your Man: The Life of Leonard Cohen* by Sylvie Simmons and immersing myself in his music, I have a different perspective. Cohen's life couldn't be more different from mine. Deeply formed in Judaism, he is the grandson of Jewish rabbis, one of whom discussed the book of Isaiah with him at night when Cohen was young. I am the daughter and wife of a Baptist minister, a mantle I have worn with some restlessness but that I have made work for me.

A wanderer around the globe, Cohen fully lived the life and the excesses of musicians of the 1960s and '70s, while I have lived within the lines of conformity all my life. I, too, am a wanderer, though, described as "defecting in place" by Sister Mary Dennison, my spiritual director. Curious and insatiable, I have read beyond the comfort zone of my critics, inviting labels that mostly make me laugh. A longtime student of a Buddhist teacher, Cohen explored beyond the confines of his tradition, and I, too, have explored beyond the boundaries of my Baptist heritage.

"It's so dark," friends commented about Cohen's last CD, *You Want It Dark*, released one week before he died, and I respond with, "Have you read the book of Lamentations in the Old Testament?"

Deep within Cohen's spiritual wisdom is the wisdom of his ancestors, sung in his magnificent "Anthem." All through his work is a profound acknowledgment of the coexistence of sorrow and joy, a recognition of the ugliness and the beauty of life, and an acceptance of what is right alongside the longing for what is not, what can't be, what used to be.

To me, Cohen's words are sweet, tender, and compassionate: "There's a crack in everything; that's how the light gets in."

I am learning this over and over: It really is through the broken places that the light of God finds a way into our darkness.

What I see and hear in the work of Leonard Cohen is that he was present to the full range of human emotion and experience, much like the writer(s) of Psalms. Cohen's refusal to ignore the darkness—in fact, his acceptance of it—actually brings it out into the light, and in exploring the depth and breadth of the human experience, he helps us embrace what we share in common: our human capacity to feel and do things that are out of sync with our highest nature and to soar to heights of ecstasy, love, and joy.

> *The sacrifices of God are a broken spirit; a broken and contrite heart.*
>
> Psalm 51:17

It was in the tradition of the Hebrew people to *lament* their losses, their sorrows, and their anger with God, and Cohen shows us what the psalmists knew. Praise is possible, but without the corresponding lament and cries of anguish for what has torn us, divided us, injured us, and often defeated us, our praise is mere escape. It is lament—the weeping of the night—that allows joy in the morning.

It is the crucifixion that allows, makes possible, brings forth resurrection.

Read the words of Cohen's music at the beginning of this chapter and see if they don't resonate with your life and, perhaps, with your regret. Better yet, find his music and listen carefully to the haunting instrumentals. Cohen labored, often for years, over this note or that one, this word or that one, aiming to coax truth out of the depths of his own heart and soul in order to evoke truth out of his listeners.

In my experience, his "Anthem" ranks close to John Newton's traditional hymn "Amazing Grace." In all of his work, Cohen seems to understand the truth we Christians proclaim when we sing, "'Twas grace that taught my heart to fear, and grace will lead me home."

We don't find hope in polishing the outsides of our cups, burnishing an image, adjusting a person, or wearing a mask to cover the truth we wish to hide from others. We find it, instead, in consciously bearing the burden of the paradox of both sides of our human nature, flesh and spirit, and admitting and knowing our brokenness and our need for healing.

It is not hiding our sin from ourselves and others that sets us free; it is bringing what is hidden out into the fresh air and the light of day that activates hope within us.

Is it easy to speak the truth about what you've done? If it's easy, it probably isn't sincere.

In my work as a spiritual director, I have sat in the symbolic sacred space while people confess, admitting their wrongs and grieving over the hurt they have inflicted on themselves and others. Usually, the confessions are made with tears of regret, shame, and guilt, but as I listen, I know their confessions are also made on a threshold of hope.

There has never been a time in these experiences when I have felt judgment toward the one who is making confession because I remember the first time I took a Fifth Step and admitted every wrong thing I had done, every harmful motivation, and every afflictive emotion I had nursed and fed in my lifetime. I remember because my Twelve Step sponsor had taken that process so seriously, and in the process, she had said two things I have never forgotten.

When I was first introduced to the Twelve Steps at age twenty-six, I had to promise my friend who had shared them with me that I would not tell anyone I had even seen them, so great was the need for those who were in either Alcoholics Anonymous or Al-Anon to keep their anonymity sacred. Since I didn't qualify for either of those recovery groups, I was not supposed to have access to the steps of the recovery process, but from the first time I read them I knew that I needed to "work the program" like my friend was working it, and I knew that the steps reflected what I had learned in Sunday school and within my lifetime of Bible studies.

Vigilantly, I worked those steps by myself on my living room couch while my infant daughter napped, and I worked them without a sponsor because, at the time, there were no recovery programs for people like me who suffered the pain of codependency. It was several years before I would learn about codependency and even more before I could convince a friend who had successfully worked the program for her alcohol addiction for many years to sponsor me. If I was going to have a sponsor, I wanted one I called a "black belt"; I wanted someone who knew what she was talking about.

I've had choices since the day that I was born.

There were voices that told me right from wrong.

If I had listened I wouldn't be here today,

Livin' and dyin' with the choices I have made.

—"Choices," Leonard Cohen

So it was that my sponsor and I met every week, and I took each step as seriously as anything I had ever done. I was fully committed to the process, and so was she, but at times she would put her head in her hands and say, "If only you were a drunk, I could help you, but until you can take [this person or that person] off the throne of your heart, there is no hope for you."

Thus, she succinctly expressed the addiction of codependency: the fact that there is always someone on the throne of your heart, someone you love and follow more than God, someone you want to please or placate or manipulate or keep calm, or some other human being to whom you give the power to make your decisions, to make you happy, to live your life for you, to determine your worth, to please you, and on and on it goes.

The difficulty of codependency is that, like work addiction, it is immediately rewarding, and when we addicts stop our people-pleasing, other people who have come to depend on our self-defeating behaviors don't like the changes we make to healthier behaviors, good boundaries, and appropriate self-care and self-compassion.

Another difficulty of codependency is that our behaviors often mask the darker motivations of afflictive emotions, so that instead of being motivated by love for the other person (which we really believe and desperately want others to believe), we are often more motivated by self-concern and even anger, hate, insecurity, guilt, or shame that we hide behind people-pleasing facades and masks.

The need to please often results from the desire to avoid another person's displeasure, and so codependents often learn to manipulate others in ways that make the love between us sticky and often toxic. There's a mixed message to codependency, a hidden agenda often hidden from ourselves but felt by others.

My sponsor plodded on with me, even as she struggled to understand the pain I had caused myself and inflicted on others. She began the work of helping me differentiate between the behaviors I had developed to keep my role as a victim, rescuer, or a persecutor and the ways I hid my real feelings behind various masks, a process I would continue in depth when I began the long and laborious journey of Jungian analysis.

"Until you can feel the deep sorrow of your harmful behaviors and be disappointed in yourself to the point of disgust, you probably aren't ready to take the Fourth and Fifth Steps," she told me, and I believed her.

I trusted her, and, in a quirky way, my people-pleasing helped me take those difficult steps of admitting my sin, confessing my sin, and becoming entirely ready for forgiveness, grace, and mercy to help me give up sinful ways that constantly separated me from God and from the people I loved most.

I didn't have any dramatic stories of conversion from a wayward life to tell. I couldn't keep up with her stories of public displays of drunkenness, but I wanted to please her so much and do the hard work she wondered if I could do that I went to work on my inner life, excavating every afflictive emotion and every hurtful deed I could in order to bring my inner darkness into the light. I wanted so much to be whole that I searched my inner motivations for the slightest duplicity and deceit, any resentment or anger, until a future spiritual director taught me that in his Catholic tradition, being *over-scrupulous* was a condition to avoid! Through it all, my people-pleasing made me work so hard, and, in that way, what Carl Jung would call my "complex" served me well.

Still, I may not like facing some inner demon, defect, or dishonesty, but the desire to be whole has been so strong that I have thus far been willing to enter the dark regions of my inner life and face what I have had to face about myself. Here's what I know about myself: I know that my codependency/people-pleasing were dishonest behaviors, fueled and fed internally by a deep pain I didn't understand for many years, a pain that I worked constantly to hide. And I know that those masks shielded a hypocrite. When the light of dawn broke on that hypocrisy, I was so disgusted I could hardly stand myself.

Unlike David, I hadn't been unfaithful to my spouse, but I had been unfaithful and dishonest to myself and to God, and in that awareness, I was deeply distressed.

That I had hurt other people out of duplicity and dishonesty, albeit unconscious to me at the time, was so disgusting that I could not wait to finish the inventory of my wrongs that I was compiling in the Fourth Step and move as quickly as I could to the Fifth.

"Remember that you take this step not as a punishment but as a way to receive forgiveness and to move forward in grace," my sponsor told me, and her eyes, her tone of voice, and her entire demeanor expressed the gravity of the moment.

But because of his great love for us, God, who is rich in mercy made us alive with Christ . . . .

Ephesians 2:4

I would love to say that my first effort at confessing my wrongs to another person was the last time I had to deal with the parts of myself that I prefer not to see. I would be happy to report that the confession was so thorough that I breezed through the next years of my life sin-free, but I learned that recovery is a lifelong project, taken one day at a time.

The hymn "Just as I Am" accompanied me through the early years of my life. After a sermon at church, there was what we called the invitation, and the message of that old hymn was so pure and simple.

> Just as I am, without one plea, but that thy blood was shed for me.
> And as thou bidst me to come to thee, O Lamb I come . . .
> Just as I am, Lord, tossed about by many a conflict and many a doubt
> Fighting fears within and without, O Lord I come . . . .

As I write, I am listening to a recording of beloved singers Willie Nelson and Johnny Cash sing this hymn of repentance and surrender. Both of these musicians were formed in Baptist spirituality, and neither of them escaped the wrestling of the body or soul any more than Leonard Cohen did.

Their voices are strong, with some rough edges like Cohen's, and I can't think of better voices to sing about the mercy of God.

> Just as I am, Lord, thou wilt receive, will welcome, pardon, cleanse, relieve.
> Because thy promise I believe, O Lamb of God, I come.

I once heard a preacher say that the church is not a museum for saints but a hospital for sinners. Having felt the burden of the pressure to *be perfect*, a condition defined by the culture of my Texas Baptist roots, I admit to the self-defeating practices of self-deception about who one really is and what one has actually done.

As my friend says, "It isn't pretty" to look square in the face of the things you wish you hadn't done or said.

Close up and personal, I knew too well the damage to the souls of people whose religion required them to polish the outside of the cup with perfect images and pristine resumes. Mistakes that were rampant among those "of the world" were not allowed, or at least not admitted, within my culture, and so the habits of hypocrisy started young.

As I look back on that culture, I see the depression among women, the rebellion among the young, and the well-earned reputation of Baptist hypocrisy. I wanted to transcend all of that so much that I began seeking the way of honesty early on, alienating people close to me along the way.

It was with an audible sigh of joy that I discovered that both Cash and Nelson, formed in what Roseanne Cash called "the mystical Baptist tradition," have also recorded Cohen's song "Bird on a Wire." It takes a special voice to sing such a bone-honest confession.

God's mercy is indeed accessible and available to those who can tell the ruthless, hard truth to themselves, admitting their failures and flaws, not to show off but to illustrate that the presence of God is alive.

In my experience, it isn't the perfect folks who speak authentically of the mercy of God; it's the ones who have gone into the depths of their dark nights of confession, just as they are, and found God.

As I see it, Leonard Cohen's "Come Healing" is as close to a hymn of invitation, an anthem of mercy, a witness to hope as any hymn I have sung in church or out.

O gather up the brokenness and bring it to now . . .
Come healing of the body; Come healing of the mind.
And let the heavens hear it, the penitential hymn;
Come healing of the spirit, Come healing of the limb.

In my childhood, we celebrated only Easter Sunday morning, often with a sunrise service and sometimes at a cemetery, which always gave me the creeps.

There was no Lent. There was no fasting, no self-examination, no place for confession. That belonged to Catholics who also kept the corpse of Jesus on the cross while we worshiped at an empty tomb and an empty cross, except we didn't allow crosses in the sanctuaries of my childhood.

There was no Maundy Thursday and no Good Friday in my childhood, but amazingly enough, it was the *soul freedom* we free Baptists so love to proclaim that led me outside the container of my childhood to explore beyond the boundaries of the past. Our beloved doctrine that asserts the priesthood of every believer, a doctrine that has been misused and misunderstood but is nevertheless precious beyond words to me, gave me an inner freedom to embrace the path of Lent, to enter into a time of self-examination and confession, and to observe in a variety of ways the sorrow of the crucifixion.

> *Leave the broken, irretrievable past in God's hands and step out into the invincible future with him.*
>
> —Oswald Chambers

In going down into my own darkness, I have touched the wellspring of mercy and the abundant fountain of hope, and maybe both are expressions of the one word that defines God: *Love*.

I find it interesting that the music of Leonard Cohen has resonated with so many Christians. Cohen, grandson of Jewish rabbis, grew up in Montreal, Canada, and was, among other things, taught the book of Isaiah by one of his grandfathers. The first time I heard him sing, I said there was something about his music that reminded me of the book of Isaiah, one of my favorite Old Testament books.

Leonard Cohen wrestled with himself and his darkness all of his life. Deep into the lifestyle of the rock and roll singers of the '60s, he lived a life vastly different from mine, but perhaps it was his sense of the reality of the Mystery of God and his struggles to accept the mercy of God that resonated with me. The boldness with which he lived his life and the depth of emotion in his music inspires me, but it also calls me to examine my own self-honesty.

Questions to Ponder

1. What is the hardest part of confession and repentance for you—seeing clearly what you have done, admitting that you can't blame anyone else because you did it, confessing to another person what you have done, or turning around and going in another direction?

2. When have you felt forgiven? What happens if you don't accept the forgiveness of God?

3. In your own experience, when has the resurrection principle been at work to make you face yourself and what you've done? What person(s) have been a part of your resurrection, new beginning, and forgiveness?

4. How do you treat your flaws? your character defects? your mistakes?

I spent my life trying to live up to
someone I thought was perfect . . .
   until someone asked me how
   that was working for me.

I spent a lot of years running from myself, trying
to hide from the fact that I believed I
was a mistake . . . that I was wrong . . .
   until someone suggested that those
   beliefs were an affront to the One
   who made me.

For too long, I believed that if I polished the
outside of my cup, my image, my persona
with good behavior, a constant smile, a
quest for perfection . . . I would make others
happier . . . I could please the ones who would
never be pleased . . .
   until someone told me that I wasn't
   created to make others happier.
God-who-made-me,
Show me the design you had in mind
when you made me . . . and help me live by it.

Chapter 10

THE HARD WAY
IS THE EASY WAY

In the tradition and tone of the Old Testament prophets, John the Baptist burst out of the wilderness with his fiery message to the Hebrew people: *Repent!*

My image of John is from the musical *Godspell* when the curtains part, the orchestra plays, and the actor playing John bursts on the screen, loudly declaring, albeit in song, "Prepare ye the way of the Lord!" I can still remember the effect that scene had on me the first time I heard it, and I get chills even now.

I can imagine how this message John proclaimed so boldly and with such authority got the attention of the people. Having lived in the desert on wild locusts and honey, surely his mannerisms were riveting and his words hard to hear. "You brood of vipers! What warned you to flee from the coming wrath? Produce fruit in keeping with repentance . . . and every tree that does not produce good fruit will be cut down and thrown into the fire" (Matt 3:7-8).

Vividly, I remember hearing the words of John the Baptist read in my church when I was a child. I also remember the extended invitations given at the end of every worship service in my childhood and adolescence. I remember my father's pleading for the souls of the people, and I remember having two-week revivals twice a year, morning and evening. Now, I reflect on those experiences with mixed feelings.

I remember the intensity of the fervent prayers of the people who asked that the lost would be convicted of their sins and finally, *finally* walk the aisle, accept Christ as personal savior, and be welcomed into the church.

When I was a teenager, a popular evangelist came to our church to conduct a revival. At the end of the week, he was not satisfied with the number of people who had "walked the aisle," the term used then to indicate a decision to accept Christ. Nor was he satisfied with the offerings for the week. The evangelist was so upset with the luke-warm response of our congregation to his zealous and loud preaching that on the last night, he ripped into our congregation, attempting to convict us of our sins. But the real motivation was not his care of our souls but his reporting to the weekly *Baptist Standard.* The better the numbers, the more invitations to other churches, and the more love offerings he would receive.

After announcing that he would be available to lead any of us who needed to be saved, the evangelist finished his rant, walked off the platform, and headed to the choir room.

Most vividly, I remember my father's rapid approach to the pulpit and his words, "Wait just a minute." He called this evangelist by name.

And then my handsome father, his black eyes lit with fire, said, "I will not allow you to talk to my people like that. These are some of the finest people on earth in this church. They are faithful Christians. They are generous, loving people who love God and love each other. They want to see people come to Christ as much as anyone, but perhaps your tactics don't match theirs."

We've seen the hubris, and now we are seeing the scandals.

—David Gergen

The silence in that sanctuary in Dallas still echoes in my memory. I was young, but I was so proud of my father.

I remember the pressure I felt as a preacher's kid to accept Christ as my personal savior, a pressure exacerbated by a few church ladies who let my dad know that it was time for his daughter to be saved and be baptized. My father didn't take well to that and let the women know that he could manage his own household and that my decision was between me and God.

Nevertheless, I remember feeling pressured to please my parents, and in my growing awareness of what it really means to become a follower of Jesus, I have changed my mind about the conversion experience, a practice Baptists hold dear. Staying out of hell and getting into heaven have been the primary reasons for many to "accept Christ."

For me, those reasons are no longer enough. I have learned that the word *eternal*, as Jesus spoke it in John 3:16, is about quality of life now, here, on earth, and not just the hereafter. Salvation, from the root word *salve*, is akin to the words "health" and "wholeness," so the fire that has fueled my passion has been about the difference a relationship with the Living Christ and the attempt to follow the teachings of the Rabbi Jesus can make in our lives here and now.

Anyone who claims to be in the light but hates his brother is still in the darkness. Whoever loves his brother lives in the light, and there is nothing in him to make him stumble. But whoever hates his brother is in the darkness and walks around in the darkness; he does not know where he is going, because the darkness has blinded him.

1 John 2:9-11

I love the idea of "inviting Jesus into my heart," and with some adult pondering and studying, I have come to understand that teaching and embrace it. I also am biased, I suppose, toward the idea of an adult conversion though I never discount the innocent trust of a child who wants to invite Jesus into her heart.

I gave as much as I understood of myself to as much as I understood of God when I was nine, and I have continued to repeat that surrender at many different stages of faith along my life's passage. As for the afterlife, I'm going to have to entrust that to the love of God.

The problem with defining the goal of salvation as staying out of hell and getting into heaven is that it often causes us to think and live as if we are "in" once we make that first confession of faith. After that, we can live any way we want to live between the present and the hereafter.

I am in no way predicting who is going to be where in the hereafter. Salvation is both event and process, and I believe the word "eternal" that John (not the Baptist but a disciple of Jesus) uses in John 3:16 to describe the gift of salvation has more to do with the quality of our lives here and now than it does the length of our lives.

Eternal life is life with God. It is a gift of grace that flows from reciprocity in God/human relationships. It is the *abundant life* of John 10:10 that Jesus came to give.

Jesus defined eternal life in John 17:3 this way: "This, then, is eternal life, that you may know me." Clearly, eternal life is about relationship with God in an intimacy as close as the vine and branches imagery Jesus used in John 15.

That relationship is to be gained by walking and talking with God and becoming familiar with who God is, especially as he is revealed in the person of Jesus. Knowledge of God is not gained by signing a card, stating that you want to be baptized, or by joining an organized church. It is not simply answering correctly the four questions of a formula.

To be a follower of Christ is to access the full splendor of God's gifts for us, and as we learn God's ways and follow the teachings of Christ, we gain knowledge.

Knowing God, then, is eternal life, and intimacy with God heals the wounded soul, transforms the willing and malleable mind and heart, and liberates us from the prisons of shame and guilt, hate and anger, inferiority and fear.

> *A recurring theme in Greek myth is the man or woman who loses sight of human limitations and acts arrogantly and with violence, as if immortal. And pays a terrible price.*
>
> —Barry B. Powell,
> *Classical Myth*

The writer of John, often called "the beloved," speaks much of love. In 1 John 4, he summarizes the relationship he described in John 15 where he calls the follower of Christ to abide (dwell, live) in Christ, promising that Christ will abide (dwell, live) in the follower. In 1 John 4:16, John begins by defining God as love in the oft-quoted verse we learned as children, "God is love." Then he immediately repeats the idea of intimacy with God in this simple statement that a child can grasp at some level, but that mystics and scholars can also spend a lifetime unpacking: "Whoever lives in love lives in God, and God in him."

If we live in God and God lives in us, John says, "In this way, love is made complete among us so that we will have confidence on the day of judgment, because in this world we are like him." Those are the words that help me let go of any worry about the afterlife. If I attempt to follow the teachings of Jesus, then I have can have confidence in God's mercy at the end of my life.

One of my favorite Scriptures follows in 1 John 4:18, and it is this: "There is no fear in love. But perfect love drives out fear."

Eugene Peterson renders these life-affirming, love-affirming words like this:

> God is love. When we take up permanent residence in a life of love, we live in God and God lives in us. This way, love has the run of the house, becomes at home and mature in us, so that we're free of worry on Judgment Day—our standing in the world is identical with Christ's. There is no room in love for fear. Well-formed love banishes fear. Since fear is crippling, a fearful life—fear of death, fear of judgment—is one not yet fully formed in love. (*The Message*, 1 John 4:17-19)

Since children have an undeveloped sense of who they are and, in Jungian terminology, of the True Self, I think it is hard to surrender one's whole life during childhood. Granted, some children have a longing for God, and I understand that intellectually and experientially. Some children, though, simply want to please their parents.

It was later in my life when I realized that, often, what brings us to the point of crying out not for resuscitation but for resurrection is an experience that also echoes the injunction of John the Baptist: *Repent.*

In *Sitting Strong: Wrestling with the Ornery God,* my book on the Old Testament story of Job, I posited the idea that there are some experiences in life so hard, so wounding, and so terrible that they could rightfully be called "Job experiences." When a Job experiences crashes into your life, you know that something has to change, that you cannot continue living the way you have lived, and that you are at the end of your ability to repair what has happened to you.

I have also suggested that certain people, events, or ideas appear— or crash—into our lives, causing us to recognize our own need for repentance. The announcement may come through an actual person, through a life-changing experience that cries out to be accepted and integrated into your life, or through recognition of an inner yearning. That John the Baptist experience may announce itself in a failure, in a life crisis, or in a recognition that you are not living the life you were made to live. That call may come to you from within. Either externally announced or internally felt, you know that you are going to have to change your mind, your heart, and your behavior.

If we claim to be without sin, we deceive ourselves and the truth is not in us. If we confess our sins, he is faithful and just and will forgive us our sins and purify us from all unrighteousness.

1 John 1:9

Carl Jung said that he calls God that which flings itself across one's path violently, for the good or for the ill. However that messenger comes, it's better to listen to the message and not wait for the volume to be increased.

When my youngest daughter, Amy, was a divinity student at Truett Seminary, she called me one day, and as we chatted, we gravitated toward a more serious topic. Whatever the topic, I'll never forget her statement: "What bothers me is when Jesus says in Matthew 7:22-23, 'Lord, Lord, did we not prophesy in your name, and in your name drive out demons and perform many miracles?' Then I will tell them plainly, 'I never knew you.'"

As people who grew up under the doctrine of "once saved, always saved," I admit that I found those words to be troubling as well. However, I keep returning to my belief that God requires of us what we see in the lives of the great biblical heroes who failed and faltered: they confessed their sins and asked for the forgiveness of God and remained in deep connection to God.

In fact, I have learned that the call to repentance, the conviction of one's own sin, and the ability to confess that sin and receive forgiveness are all inspired and empowered by the presence and activity of God. It is as if God quickens our minds and hearts to see what we have done and to be courageous enough to face our darkest deeds. It is God, I believe, who loves us enough to make our regret and sorrow for what we have done strong enough that we repent—turn and go in a new direction.

Have mercy on me, O God, according to your unfailing love; According to your great compassion, blot out my transgressions. Wash away my iniquity and cleanse me from every sin. For I know my transgressions, and my sin is ever before me. Against you and you only have I sinned and done what is evil in your sight.

Psalm 51:4

God is the giver of forgiveness, the source of grace, mercy, and peace, and it seems that our impulse to cry out to him is a response to his constant, unrelenting love toward us.

I never conjecture about the afterlife and don't listen to those who think they have it figured out. I'm going to have to let that rest in the hands of God. I operate with the definition of sin being separation from God; so it seems that since God is always present and always wanting the intimacy described in the image of the vine and the branches in John 15, I must do my part to keep the connection with God. I must allow God's will and presence to flow into me and into the fruit that is consistent with who I am.

A call to repentance is first a call to repair or restore my connection with God. Even my feelings of guilt over a wrong action or my neglect of the covenant relationship with God are evidence of the resurrection principle. The voice of God within awakens me and moves me to repentance.

Human hubris: In Greek tragedy, an excess of ambition, pride or arrogance, ultimately causing the transgressors ruin.

If I have been consistently faithful to God, then a call to repentance, whether it comes from an inner unrest or an outer conflict, is a call to go deeper with God. How that is worked out in everyday life is different for different people.

Repentance: Deep sorrow, contrition, regret for a past sin, wrongdoing or action. Metanoia (Greek) indicates a radical change, a turning around and going in the opposite direction, a change of mind, purpose and life.

After the call to repentance comes, there is a necessary self-examination or, as the Twelve Steps say it, we are called to do a "fearless and searching moral inventory." The other definition of sin is an archery term, "missing the mark." Doing a self-examination or moral inventory has the benefit and grace of showing us where we are missing the mark of God's intent for our life, whether that is in how we think or what we do.

Missing the mark can be a defiance of God's laws, a willful turning away from God, or an intentional violation of another person. It can be a moral failure, an ethical transgression, or a refusal to be and become the person you are created to be and to do what you were sent here to do.

In the Yokefellow spiritual growth groups, we learned to differentiate the sins of behavior, action, or word from the motivating Sins that originate within. We defined the capital-S sins as fear, guilt, and shame, a sense of inferiority or inadequacy, hate, and anger, and referred to them as inner demons.

Those inner demons, Sins, manifested themselves in behavior. To get to the cause of a problem in the outer world, we were asked to identify that problem, and then track it back to the cause, which was usually one of the inner demons. Confessing the cause, addressing the motivation for the behavior, and taking responsibility for how that demon was self-sabotaging or hurtful to others were the beginning steps of getting to the source of the problem. Addressing only the symptoms—the outward behaviors—was only the beginning of release from the problem.

The Yokefellow idea is that attempting to change the outer behavior without identifying the inner demon misses the mark. It is the failure to root out the cause of the moral failure, the character defect, or the behaviors that separate us from God, from the True Self, and from others.

As a student at the Jung Center in Houston, Texas, I heard both Pittman McGehee and Jim Hollis, Jungian analysts, authors, and lecturers, say that "the one thing the gods would not tolerate was *human hubris*."

Sometimes *hubris* is related to ignorance or a lack of knowledge, and it generally implies that suffering or punishment will follow the ones who cannot release their pride and repent. Worse still, the one who is consumed with hubris usually cannot even see his own hubris and therefore cannot admit it, confess it, or repent of it.

Hubris makes us want to be like God, to be worshiped and adored, to be followed and set up on a high and mighty throne of admiration. Hubris makes us neglect or ignore the laws of God and seduces us into thinking we are above the law or can buy their way around the laws. Sometimes people can get by with what they do for a long time, and sometimes they *can* buy their way out.

Eventually, though, we reap what we sow, and while the crop may be a long time coming in, it finally appears.

I don't want to be consumed by hubris. I don't *want* to face my inner demons that cause harm to others and to myself. I don't *want* to violate the laws of God and turn away from his love and his purpose, but when I do, I know there is a way back.

Repentance is the key to forgiveness.

Repentance is a first step in practicing resurrection.

Repentance restores hope because repentance is filled with the mercy and grace of God.

There are problems with repentance, however, and I would be foolish to overlook the ways we avoid this powerful and healing spiritual practice, which sets us free to experience inner freedom, grace, and peace.

It is a problem when a person cannot bring himself to see his own sin.

It is a problem when a person cannot say, "I'm sorry."

It is a problem when a person excuses, justifies, or rationalizes what she has done.

It is a problem when a person feels no need of forgiveness.

It is a problem when a person feels no need for repentance.

It is a problem when one is too proud or arrogant to ask for forgiveness.

These are problems human beings generate; they are barriers to knowing God and living in a dynamic, personal relationship with God.

The relationship we have with God will be lived out in our human relationships. Note that the first four of the Ten Commandments are about the God-person relationship, and the last six are about our relationships with other humans.

It is also true that how we treat other people and how we treat ourselves reveals who we believe God to be.

The process of repentance is simple, but it is not always easy. As the Twelve Step slogan puts it, "The hard way is the easy way."

This process begins with recognition of what is separating you from God, which may be reflected in a separation with another human being.

You go on to practice self-awareness, identifying the feeling—one of the Yokefellow "demons" described above in this chapter—and owning up to the fact that you have the feeling that led to whatever regretful thing you are doing or did.

Repentance is possible when you say, "I did this. No one made me do it. I blame no one, and I take full responsibility for the wrong I have done and the harm I have inflicted on others."

Repentance is not remorse. It may begin with remorse and regret, but those responses may mean only "I wish no one knew" or "I'm sorry I got caught." Repentance says, "I want to go another way. This is not how I want to live, how I want to behave, how I want to feel," and then goes another step that leads to confession, first to God and then, when appropriate, to another human being.

> *1, even 1, am he who blots out your transgressions, for my own sake, and remembers your sins no more.*
>
> Isaiah 43:25

God is eager to forgive us and help us turn our lives around, and he seems to know when we are ready for a fresh beginning, a resurrection.

A consistent practice of self-examination—knowing yourself, paying attention to what you have done or are doing that is out of sync with God's love, and confessing and asking for forgiveness—is part of *practicing resurrection.*

Self-examination is not self-torture. It is examining yourself in order to be set free of what binds you. Self-examination is practicing resurrection in that it opens the pathways for grace and mercy to flow.

In the oddest of ways, hitting bottom can be the beginning of new life.

Being brought to the end of your ability to manage your own character defect, accepting the ways in which hubris is ruining your life, identifying your guilt and shame, hate and anger, inferiority or fear, and being willing to have God remove those shortcomings and fill your mind and heart with his love are part of the spiritual path of practicing resurrection.

Questions to Ponder

1. How do you deal with what you have done to hurt another person?
    I don't like to think about it. (Avoidance)
    It wasn't that bad. (Denial)
    He made me do it. (Blame)
    Look what he did! (Projection)
    The reason I did it was . . . . (Justification)
    I wouldn't have done it, but . . . . (Rationalization)
    I did it. (Admission)
    I am sorry. (Apology)
    I won't do it again. (Repentance)
    I will fix what I have broken. (Making Amends)

2. How does prayer fit in with your practices of self-examination, confession, and repentance?

3. When have you felt the life-giving relief of admitting the exact nature of your wrong?

4. What has been your experience of confessing and being forgiven?

5. What happens when you repress or suppress your afflictive emotions?

God, you have heard my prayer of confession.
    Through your human instruments,
    you have spoken words of forgiveness.
Thank you for your mercy.

Loving God, you have rescued me
    from the pit of self-condemnation.
    You have restored my soul.
Thank you for your compassion.

Eternal Love, you have shown me the
    way of grace, and by your Mystery
    you have gone deep into my inner
    kingdom to places in myself that
    I cannot see, and you have
repaired what I didn't know was broken,
liberated what I didn't know was trapped,
transformed that which was not enough,
and empowered that which had no strength.

By your grace
you have healed me by your forgiveness.
    Great Physician, in your gracious economy
    use my wounds to heal others.
    Use me, if you can, as your instrument.

Chapter 11

CHANGING DIRECTIONS

Always, after the celebrations and observances of Advent and Christmas, Lent and Easter, I ask myself what difference such rituals make in the way I live. What actual difference do the Incarnation and Resurrection make?

Often, I examine my own life in a kind of integrity checkup, asking myself how and if I am walking my talk. When I identify as a *Christian*, how am I doing at following the teachings of Jesus? Is my intention to be conformed to his image consistent with my conversations, my judgments and discernment, my behavior?

I don't ask myself those questions to feel guilty or to self-punish. I ask them because I believe that when it comes to following Jesus, bringing my thoughts, feelings, actions, and affections into harmony is important.

Accepting Christ as my personal savior and being baptized at nine years old are important parts of my story, but

> *Insanity is doing the same thing over and over and expecting a different result.*
>
> —Anonymous

if they were the only effort I made toward what Paul calls "working out my salvation," my inner growth would be stunted. At nine, I didn't have either the understanding or the capacity for self-examination, and I hadn't strayed from God, broken his laws, or committed serious offenses against God or others. I had to grow into my rebellion, and that took growing older!

Just as the vow I made at the marriage altar was only the beginning, my early acceptance of Christ was only the beginning. We do newcomers in the faith and children a grave disservice when we do not mentor or sponsor them diligently, helping them grow into faith.

I have come to love the Greek word *metanoia*, which means a profound inner transformation, a changing of directions, a thorough and basic change of thoughts. We use the word *repentance* lightly, but an examination of its roots in the Greek word *metanoia* elevates the practice of simply acknowledging my sins to a redirection of my whole life, oriented around the teachings of Jesus and the grace and mercy of the Living Christ. Transformation, I have learned, happens layer by layer, one day at a time.

Sometimes, when teaching my adult Bible study class or leading a retreat or workshop, I like to stir the waters a bit, asking questions such as the following.

When someone joins a Christian church, is the shared assumption that the person is a follower of Jesus? Do we ever wonder if this person has experienced a changed life because of his relationship with Christ?

Is there a difference between a church member and a disciple?

If we are to "work out our salvation with fear and trembling," as Paul teaches in Philippians 2:12, what does that mean? Can't we go on living our lives as we always have?

If I give my heart to Jesus, join a church, and then continue to live my life as I did before with no particular thoughts about that relationship aside from my days of occasional church attendance, am I still saved? Is going to heaven when I die the only benefit of salvation?

Does it matter how I act or feel or think in everyday life if I know I am going to heaven when I die?

A person from another denomination asked if I would lead a six-week study for women on the topic of "Christian womanhood." I had to ask her for clarity because that terminology may mean one thing to one person and something entirely different to another.

A person from yet another denomination asked if I would lead a retreat on "Establishing Our Christians Goals," and a third asked me to speak on being a "Christian writer."

When I was growing up, I assumed that when someone identified as a Christian, I knew what that meant. In my adulthood, I have learned that a person can identify as a Christian when she is actually using the term as an association with a particular political party or the plank of a political party's platform. Some people impose political ideas onto the word "Christian" without considering that a political definition is almost alien to the teachings of Jesus. Over the years, I have learned to ask people to tell me more clearly what they want when they ask me to speak about "Christian" things.

To others, being "Christian" may imply certain social norms that belong to a denomination or even a region of the country or world. For example, some believe that being a Christian means that you must not drink alcohol or dance, while others do that freely. Some believe that you must renounce worldly wealth, dress a particular way, or follow particular rules, rituals and rites in order to be a Christian.

I was asked to speak at a banquet close to Easter by a group from a mainline, Protestant church. A few weeks before the event, I received a call from the chair of the group, who told me clearly and directly that they knew I was Baptist and hoped I would not talk about "that Jesus stuff" in my speech.

We cannot solve today's problems with the same level of thinking that created them.

—Albert Einstein

Today on the radio I heard a Syrian Christian woman describing meetings of Christian women in conflict-ridden, war-torn Syria. At first I had a compassionate response toward the story, but then I was surprised when the woman said, "Of course, not all of them are believers; they just want to identify as Christian." It took my breath away, not because I hadn't ever imagined such a thing but because I see that very tendency in my own country.

Because of all of those factors, I continue to be passionate about sharing the life and teachings of Jesus. Since he is the founder of our faith we call Christianity, I need to know what it is he said and did not say if I am going to attempt to follow him.

Along the way, I have had to continue to explore and challenge what I call my *integrity of faith* issues, a process that includes checking the places where my walk doesn't match my talk and the areas of my thinking that lead me to easy "believism." In following Jesus, it isn't a matter of *if it feels good, it must be good.*

With gratitude to my friends who introduced me to the Twelve Steps for recovering addicts, codependents, and others whose recalcitrant ways have led us away from God instead of toward God, I have had to recognize that following Jesus is far more than inviting him into my heart. Following the teachings of Jesus and developing a personal, dynamic love relationship with the Living Christ challenges my integrity over and over.

Even though I have "been a Christian" since I was nine years old, my spiritual path has not been a linear journey. I have changed directions, made mid-course corrections, and sometimes cycled back to retrieve something I lost. My spiritual

> *No one sews a patch of unshrunk cloth on an old garment, for the patch will pull away from the garment, making the tear worse. Neither do men pour new wine into old wineskins. If they do, the skins will burst, the wine will run out and the wineskins will be ruined. No, they pour new wine into new wineskins, and both are preserved.*
>
> Matthew 9:16-18

path has been a circuitous journey similar the path of the Chartres labyrinth when, sometimes, while following the path with focus and intention, I have found myself close to the center and then, suddenly, out on the edge.

If I take my commitment to Christ seriously, my relationship with him is more like allowing him to move into my heart and cause a radical reformation, a reorienting of my life around his designs and a re-creation of my way of being in the world.

The recovering people I have been privileged to know talk about making a radical change of life if you want to stay sober. You cannot, I learned, put one foot in the water and hold another one on dry land if you are serious about being healed of your addiction.

Twelve Step people are so serious about the gravity of this process of change and recovery that they even talk about egocide, which sounds frightening; it is frightening if you understand ego as the way you think you are or the way you have always been. If we see the ego as the outer appearance we present to the world and the roles, personas, masks, and images we project to others, then we can truthfully say that we all have ego.

In a process of recovery, however, or in the working out of our salvation, we come face to face with the truth that the way we think we are and the ways that have always worked for us have to be sacrificed. Egocide is the moment when we let go of the ways that have gotten us into the plight we are in and reach out for instructions for what it means to be what Paul calls "a new creation."

In the Christian tradition, the process of transformation begins with repentance, which is far more than remorse. "Being sorry" may be where one begins, but the real work of healing and transformation begins when we come face to face with what we have done, who we have become, and how we have affected other people in such a way that we are truly sorry.

True redemption is possible when we fall from grace in our own eyes to such a degree that we know *something has to change.*

"You don't understand; walking with you through your journey helps me. It shows me that I am not alone on my path, and I learn from you, my companion on the way." Those tender words brought tears to my eyes and showed me how much we need each other as we move forward, beckoned by the love of the Living Christ and pushed from behind by our restlessness, our pain, our yearning to be free.

My Thursday Morning Bible Study women are smart and savvy and often sassy, and I value their wisdom and insight, their quick wit, their questions and responses. They are curious and unafraid to ask hard questions, and we have walked through some of life's big challenges together over twenty-five years. More than anything, I treasure their faithfulness to God and to each other.

Facilitating this topic, "Practicing Resurrection," in a yearlong Bible study with them was challenging, but it was encouraging, inspiring, and helpful to me because of who they are. Writing the book has been a different experience because of events in the world and in the lives of people I love and in the personal shifts and changes in my own life.

Because recent world and national events have shaken the foundations and institutions of my culture and because of radical changes in my life, I decided that if I was going to take on the challenge of writing about keeping hope alive in a world that seems at times to be conspiring against hope, I would do two things.

First, because hope is a spiritual quality, I doubled down in my efforts to go deeper in my spiritual practices that nurture, support, and encourage the inward gift of hope. Centering Prayer, time for solitude and reflection, reading to nurture my soul, and practicing the Eleventh Step of AA to "improve my conscious contact with God" became the stabilizing practices necessary to keep hope alive internally.

You cannot grow to a new level of faith without your current level of faith being challenged.

—Thomas Keating

Second, I balanced this inward focus on hope with attention to an outward focus: while I was writing this book, I looked for signs of hope in the outer world, and I was astounded. I came across positive newspaper articles and anecdotes from friends about something good they had seen or done. Small moments of connections with strangers or the kind words people said to each other popped up unbidden in the common, ordinary paths of daily life. Grace-gifts, I called them, given to encourage and inspire hope.

In late winter and early spring 2017, I heard the words "I have lost hope" countless times. I know of more suicides in this last year than I have known before, and I cry out, "God, what can we do to keep hope alive?" The answer continues to be, "Draw near to God" and "Open your eyes and see!"

Pushed to the extreme, others have begun rising up and speaking up within the chaos of the times and on behalf of possibility and promise, potential and personal empowerment, and I see that as good news. I'm reading that some parts of the Christian church, perhaps alarmed by the despair of the culture and the decline in church attendance, are growing. Progressives, I hear, are returning to church.

"What are our choices?" one of my strong friends asked of a group of us. "We can sit and snivel, or we can stand up and do something that is right and true and *life-giving*."

I've noticed, however, that when I take the high road in anything, whether it is forming a new, healthy habit, reaching out in love to someone, or living with hope, the other side of life seems to get a notice to rise up and try to prove me wrong about my good intentions.

"There's sand in every oyster," a friend tells me. It's true, but that's what makes the pearl.

So it is that I have learned to watch for the pearl in the deepest pain.

"I don't even know what you mean when you talk about hope. I don't think I have any hope, and I thought I was a Christian!"

Those words were punctuated with bitter tears. The strong and capable person sitting before me could represent many people with whom I have had the privilege of sharing the holy process of spiritual direction.

Those words pulled on my heartstrings and activated memories and a strong sense of empathy. I could have said those words at certain times in my life. Thankfully, there have been people who have sat quietly with me while I wrestled with hopelessness.

In the aftermath of the 2016 presidential election, many people expressed deep feelings that went far beyond mere disappointment in the outcome. Many expressed sorrow and regret that family members and friends were so polarized that they couldn't talk to each other. Some were shocked at the force with which both sides defended their candidate, often resorting to harsh words or convoluted arguments to prove a point. Others were alarmed at the increase in public rudeness and obscenities and violence.

The issues went beyond the ordinary responses to who won and who lost. Deeper than that, some wept while reflecting on what has been described as "the deep divide" in the country that is experienced as a chasm between friends and family members.

"Why can't we talk about this without insulting each other or getting mad?" people asked, often through tears.

On the occasion I described above and with the person who had come to the end of a rope, I took deep breaths and prayed for guidance in choosing my words. I also prayed for the wisdom and skill to differentiate my responses as the spiritual director from my directee's responses. It is important to me that I enter into the reality of my directee without projecting my experience, feelings, or opinions onto the other person. Together, we are to discern what the real director, the Holy Spirit, is attempting to do in the life—both inner and outer—of the directee.

The liberating truth about walking with others through various valleys of dark shadows is that I don't have to figure out another person's life, and it isn't my place to say, "This is what you ought to do." It is my job to listen to the cries of the human heart and the guidance of God and to give support, often by silence and presence and sometimes by words, to the seeker who has entrusted an open or a broken heart to me.

There was a time when I thought it was my job to give a pep talk or at least some holy encouragement to people who were feeling disappointment, dread, or despair. Early on, I wanted to help, whether the problem was a current crisis, feelings of apathy and indifference, or the condition described by a little-used word today, *acedia*. This Greek term is used to describe a kind of listlessness or lifelessness, dissatisfaction, or inertia. It is not exactly depression because there is the element of willful cooperation and choice with the state of acedia, a choice that hovers close to sloth or laziness. In some ways, acedia is to one's spiritual health what depression is to one's mental health.

Considered a sin in monastic life and brought to consciousness by Kathleen Norris in her book *Acedia and Me: A Marriage, Monks, and a Writer's Life*, acedia can manifest as excessive sleepiness and the inability to perform one's duties or even take steps to live one's daily life. While it seems to come over you like the flu, it is often possible, with self-honesty and reflection, to wake up to the ways in which you may collude with acedia.

As a spiritual director, I walk a fine line in discerning whether a professed loss of hope is within the boundaries of spiritual direction or if it is a psychological issue. If the issue is psychological, I refer individuals to outstanding professionals. I have strong boundaries when it comes to what I can do and what I must not do.

> *Jesus said, no procras-tination. No backward looks. You can't put God's kingdom off until tomorrow. Seize the day.*
>
> Luke 9:62,
> *The Message*

Listening deeply, it is my job to ask whether the symptom is being confused with a grief process or if it is an avoidance of God, a state of being that is common among even the most serious seekers of a deeper, more passionate, more faithful relationship with God, who is often most elusive when we seek him most fervently.

I've learned to ask questions when people confess a loss of hope, and I have learned to pay attention when I feel myself turning toward disappointment, despair, discouragement, or situational depression. As a spiritual director and as a seeker, I need to remember that acedia is the natural result of turning away from God's love, a common tendency of those of us who attempt to follow him.

However, it is never my job to criticize someone for "sliding into" despair or acedia. It is not my intention—ever—to shame a person for feeling hopeless. I know how it feels to be told, "You shouldn't feel that way!"

I have learned how to sit with people who are in devastating emotional and spiritual pain. Fortunately, I have had wonderful teachers show me how to bear others' burdens without either taking them on as mine or brushing them away. By others' examples, I know how to walk with people through the deep valleys of the shadows of death and dying.

I know the stages of grief not as orderly stages that we can check off one at a time but as states of being through which the bereaved cycle. Grief lasts as long as it takes for the grieving person to come to the place of acceptance. The grief process is unpredictable and circular rather than linear.

When it came to my own first big loss, however, my head knowledge was not enough to sustain me through the long winter that followed the events that turned my world upside down. My ability to be comforting to others may have made me understand what was happening now and then, but the truth is that my first big loss introduced me to the debilitating force of hopelessness.

I know what it is like to have to give up on a particular outcome or on a preconceived notion of how life is going to be. I know what it's like to give up hope when it is clear that someone is not going to survive an illness or when a marriage is going to fail. I know what it is like to sit with a parent whose child has rejected him, and I know how it feels to give up hope that someone who should have loved you doesn't.

In looking back at the various confessions of losing hope, it is interesting to remember that in confessing a loss of hope, every person seemed to have an overlay of guilt. "I know that as a Christian, I shouldn't say this, but . . . ." "I know you're going to think I'm awful, but . . . ." "I don't know what's happening to me, and it scares me to death, but I don't know if there is a God anymore!" These are natural laments, honest admissions, and, in a sense, courageous statements of faith.

Remember this one: "My God, my God, why have you forsaken me?"

Spoken through his agony on the cross, these words show that even Jesus had the experience of feeling that God had abandoned him. We, lesser mortals, naturally have those terrifying moments when we lose hope or faith and believe for a moment or a season that God has abandoned us.

The hesitation to confess our lack of faith connects to the force of *acedia*, and I have learned that the concept of acedia helps us cope with the feeling of hopelessness and turn back to hope.

We don't deny the feelings of hopelessness or despair. Knowing that whatever we resist persists, I have learned that being mindful of those feelings is a step toward hope. The object of my hope has to be in God alone, not in an outcome, and I have also had to learn when it's time to give up hope in a particular outcome or desire. Try as I may to give up my attachment

> *To awaken others to the hope that is in them may be the greatest thing we can do for them.*
>
> —E. Glenn Hinson

to a parrticular outcome, and as fervently as I believe that hope in God is the way of peace, there are times when my humanity runs ahead of my intentions.

Honoring the feelings I don't want to feel and relating to those feelings with self-compassion are steps in the process of moving from darkness back into the light of hope. It may take several attempts to surrender the hopelessness to God and wait in the darkness of despair with the intention of moving into hope. It may take several bouts of wrestling with the angels of fear or anxiety and the willingness to be radically honest about our feelings to come to the place of being able to accept the things we cannot change.

"I am afraid to feel how bad I feel," a person told me, and because I understood, I did not run away by trying to talk her into feeling better.

"I will be with you," I told her. "I am not afraid of your feelings."

Feelings are powerful and strong, and sometimes they overwhelm us. They may reflect an outer reality or hard facts to face, but suppressing or repressing them doesn't make them go away. What is buried alive stays alive, so I have come to see that through compassion to ourselves, acceptance, and kind and loving presence, we learn to surrender our wild and chaotic feelings to God. Surrender itself is a spiritual practice, and, like all practices, we get better at surrender.

We practice the new behaviors—changes in attitude and mindsets that we want in our lives—not by wrestling with our wild and chaotic thoughts and feelings but by admitting them and asking God to replace them with his love. We work out our salvation by doing spiritual practices, and sometimes we tremble.

If it takes a lifetime to perfect the qualities we want to manifest in our lives, so what? It takes as long as it takes, and if we can be as patient with ourselves as we are with a yearling learning to walk or as patient as God is with us, we will have the energy we need to be persistent.

The twin gremlins of anxiety and despair await all of us each day, but so does the opportunity to choose courage and peace. We practice resurrection not just now and then, but daily.

Each time I return to a position of hopefulness, I am reminded of the gracious words of Thomas Keating about the challenges of learning how to handle distractions, physical restlessness, mind-wandering, troubling memories, or the omnipresent to-do list, all of which are interruptions we call "thoughts" in the practice of Centering Prayer.

"Every time your mind wanders or something distracts you," Keating would say to us, "be grateful that you have another opportunity to learn how to return to your sacred word."

Unless we just sit and rock on the porches of our lives, our faith and hope will be challenged. Wavering and wobbling in that journey doesn't mean we have lost hope or that God has abandoned us. Perhaps we are being called to a deeper level of intimacy with the

One who dwells within, offering hope and help, grace and mercy from an unending supply.

When I was growing up, paintings of Bible stories hung on the walls of my Sunday school classes. One that always fascinated me was the picture of Jesus outside a door, knocking. I can remember hearing someone talk about how there was no handle on the door, so the only way to open the door was from within.

The picture from my childhood was painted by Warner Sallman, and it made an indelible impression on me. Today, I treasure a print of the contemporary artist Greg Olsen titled "Let Him In."

In the early-morning darkness of my study, I sat in my chair for my practice of Centering Prayer, journaling, and reading. Normally, I begin this time of spiritual practice with Centering Prayer, but, feeling tossed about by uncertainties of the future and the ragged edges of a busy weekend, I turned first to the daily reading in this year's edition of *Sacred Space*, a prayer book prepared by the Irish Jesuits. There, at the beginning of the day's readings, was the Scripture that inspired the many paintings of Jesus, knocking on the door with no outer handle. "Here I am! Behold I stand at the door and knock. If anyone hears my voice and opens the door, I will come in and eat with him, and he with me" (Rev 3:20).

I almost gasped, and then I had to smile.

When I am tossed about by fear, heavy with worries, consumed by my own agendas, I can drift into hopelessness or despair.

Sitting there in the dark, however, I smiled because it occurred to me that the very things that I worry about—the disruptive feelings of guilt or anger, my tendency to feel inadequate, or anything that separates me from a sense of the Presence of God—can be seen as a knock on the door and a plea from the Living Christ to let him in!

If I don't fight these distractions, they are, as Keating taught us, opportunities for returning to my sacred word, an affirmation of my faith in God.

Just as the sacred word I use in Centering Prayer expresses my consent to the presence and action of Christ in my mind, my heart, my inner kingdom, my secret room, my unconscious, so can the troubles of my outer world be interpreted and understood as the knock on the door, beckoning me to turn within, access the presence of God within, and offer once again my heart to be the dwelling place of the origin of hope itself.

The practices of the contemplative life are indeed mysterious because the mere possibility of having a dynamic, personal love relationship with the Unseen One is mysterious. Encountering God, abiding in Christ, and being filled with the Holy Spirit are all about engagement with the Mystery, and therefore they are impossible to define or fully explain.

Maintaining hope in the presence of what seems hopeless seems impossible, but from my own life, I know this to be true: spiritual practice does not guarantee a spiritual experience, but it can make you more available to the possibility.

The effects of spiritual practice are not ego building, and in fact, the effect is the dismantling of the ego's defenses. Spiritual practice operates at the unseen level, and so it is soul-nourishing and strengthening. When done faithfully, spiritual practice, whether it is meditation, spiritual reading, Bible study, or journaling, builds hope. It promotes a growing conscious contact with God, which in turn produces change from within.

On a crisp summer morning in Lake City, Colorado, we bundled up our little girls and joined a caravan of assorted vehicles for a daylong adventure into the high country.

Guided by our friend Frank Pool, we drove above the timberline where the sky was bright blue. We turned off the paved roads and onto the ever-narrowing dirt roads, bouncing along until we got to a place where there were no roads at all. For the life of me, I couldn't understand how our leader knew how to find our destination without a clear path, but I trusted him.

The higher we went, the colder it got. "It seems that if we are getting closer to the sun, it should be getting warmer," one of my children mused, squinting in the bright sun.

Finally, the lead vehicle indicated that we had arrived, and so we all pulled in behind him, one by one, and piled out onto the rocks. What I didn't realize was that "arriving" was just the beginning of another part of our adventure.

Stretching after the bumpy ride, we loaded up with fishing gear, blankets, and our lunches and started out, only to be stopped short when we saw our destination below us.

There in the high country, nestled among majestic trees, reflecting perfectly the few white clouds drifting calmly above it was Heart Lake. I will never forget my first glimpse of the pristine beauty of Heart Lake below us. And I mean *below* us.

Nor will I forget the realization that if we wanted to fish in the lake or simply bask in the beauty of the place, we had to get down a steep mountain.

IFrank was our guide, and, quickly, he all but scampered down that mountain to the lake, scoping out the best fishing spots. We, on the other hand, started down the mountain slowly and with hesitation. Determined, we kept moving toward the water, but when fear of the steep descent and the cold finally overwhelmed our youngest daughter, she wailed. Frankly, I wanted to cry with her. The way to the destination seemed too perilous, too hard, too steep for her five-year-old courage and my nerves.

> *There is nothing more difficult yet more gratifying in our society than living with sincere, active, constructive hope for the human spirit.*
>
> —Maria Popova

In a flash, Frank Pool was back up the mountain and heading for my child. "You can do this!" he told her, taking her by her hand and showing her how to sidestep down the mountain. "Come on. I know you can do this," he said several times, encouraging her with every step and never, not once, letting go of her hand or giving in to her fears.

The man who took my little girl's hand was a World War II veteran. Part of the Greatest Generation, he had fought in the European theater of that awful war, and he carried in his body shrapnel as souvenirs. That tall, bold man had built a big business, and he had also faced untold personal challenges and tragedies; he knew what it was like to look fear and hardship, loss and sorrow in the face. He also knew what it took to succeed and what it meant to lend a firm hand to those who needed to be guided through dark valleys of fear.

That big man got my little girl to the bottom of the hill and watched her scamper and play on the more level ground, and from then on, he and my children were bonded.

Always an optimist and an encourager, Frank was an innovator and engineer, a major force in the oil business of West Texas and far beyond, a school board member and champion of integration. All of his endeavors were sustained by a longtime faithfulness to his church in San Angelo, Texas, and by the joys of his wife and their children, grandchildren, and great-grandchildren. Once you were a friend of Frank Pool, you were a forever friend.

In the last years of his life, Frank Pool's indomitable spirit was strong even when his short-term memory failed. When I called him or when his daughters or friends stopped by, his constant question was, "What are you going to do now?" or "What are you doing next?" Always and to the end of his life, Frank's direction was in a forward motion, powered by hope and supported by his ultimate faith and trust in God's redeeming love.

As I was finishing writing this book, our friend died at age ninety-eight, and our sense of loss was deep. When we who loved him gathered to say one final goodbye, my memory of that cold, sunny morning in Colorado when he taught my child to make it down a steep mountain came to me over and over.

Frank Pool was a hero to my family and to me for many reasons over a lifetime of friendship, and when he was gone, I had a wrenching longing for him to come and hold our hands and help us down the steep mountain of grief.

We honor his memory, though, by holding hands, young and old, and pushing through our fears to live in courage and hope on the inevitable rocky and steep paths of life.

With a deep faith in God, Frank Pool taught me how to look for what's next, to live with hope, and now I must remember to pass on to others the transforming grace of hope.

Frank's faith forged the stamina and strength necessary for the challenges of life. His firm belief in the presence and action of God nurtured his soul through the hard times and gave him the ability to persevere and to hope.

Frank became a source of hope for countless family and friends not by staying safe in a warm cocoon but by living on the cutting edges of adventure and then by allowing us to learn from him and, when necessary, lean on him.

The resurrection principle at work in him nourished the life force in all of us who were privileged to call him friend.

Questions to Ponder

1. Who in your history modeled a commitment to the way of Christ? What effect did that have on you?

2. In your experience, how strong is the connection between your commitment to Christ and the presence of hope in you?

3. When have you decided to turn from one way of living and begin living another? How did this turning affect the presence of hope in you?

4. In what ways do you practice resurrection?

What will it cost me to
    practice resurrection? What
    does that mean for me, anyway? What will
    it cost me if I don't make the turn?
    Will I have to change my point
of view about life and
God or current events?
    What will it mean for me
    to practice resurrection in the
    ways I talk to others,
    the topics I think about,
    the way I treat those whose
        services I need?
When I am feeling low or
anxious, what will I have to
change in order to practice resurrection?
Will I still numb myself with television?
Will I distract myself, medicate myself to
    get through an evening?
    Will I work too hard, live
in excesses, try to please too much?
Loving God, I want the new plan.
I want to live as if I believe in you . . . Help me turn the
corner, please.

Chapter 12

THE POWER OF A GREAT AFFECTION

"This Jesus stuff won't work in real life. You'd be run over out in the real world!"

Whether I'm traveling or teaching adults in my own church, I'm used to being interrupted by statements such as these, and I always stop and take a deep breath and let the words of the speaker reverberate in the room.

"You can't expect us to take these teachings into everyday life. People would think we don't know how to play the games of corporate life!"

Actually, I love it when those outbursts and challenges come while I am sharing anything about the life and teachings of Jesus. Usually, I pause and give the protestor my undivided attention and hope the rest of the class can relax. Though many in the group I'm leading may be thinking the same thing as the person who dares to challenge Jesus' words, they may think I am going to be threatened by the challenge. I'm used to it!

"I didn't know you had to do all of this to be a Christian!" one weary newcomer in the faith declared. "I thought all you had to do was accept Christ!"

I've written three books on the life and teachings of Jesus, and the deeper I have gone into the Jesus story, the more convinced I have become of two important realities that have led me to make a commitment to teaching and writing about the centrality of Christ. He is, after all, the founder of the faith we Christians proclaim.

One of the realities I have discovered is that many people who check *Christian* on a hospital or census form may know very little about what Jesus actually taught and said—and what he did not teach or say. The second reality is that many people who attend church may not differentiate between the traditions, rituals, and social mores of their particular church, the doctrines taught by that church, and the actual teachings of Jesus because in many churches, that teaching has been left behind. I am happy when someone gives me the opportunity to make some distinctions and, perhaps, heighten awareness of what it means to be a follower of Jesus.

But what happens when we live God's way? He brings gifts into our lives, much the same way that fruit appears in an orchard—things like affection for others, exuberance about life, serenity. We develop a willingness to stick with things, a sense of compassion in the heart, and a conviction that a basic holiness permeates things and people. We find ourselves involved in loyal commitments, not needing to force our way in life, able to marshal and direct our energies wisely.

Galatians 5:22-23,
The Message

Beginning where most of the people who gather in my classes or on retreats are, I talk about what I call the "rules of the road" or the rules of engagement for our everyday lives. While I may begin the list, others typically add rules I had not considered, but basically, what I have discovered is that these are the rules that govern our culture:

- Compete and defeat.
- Win at all costs.
- The end justifies the means.
- Take care of number one.
- Don't let them see you cry.
- Don't ever say you're sorry.
- Numb your feelings. Distract yourself from your pain.

Once I start articulating the rules of everyday engagement, the room gets quiet. Stressed and pushed and prodded to live under the strain of *getting there*, most of us feel the pressures to succeed; to be perfect parents, or to be thin enough, powerful enough, rich enough, and well-connected enough. Those stresses begin early and last long, usually until something—health, a marriage, a kid's trouble or even suicide, or a moral, financial, physical, or emotional breakdown—stops the tedious trajectory of pursuing the American dream.

Pausing to switch gears, I list some of the teachings of Jesus.

- Come to me, and I will give you rest.
- Abide in me, and I will abide in you.
- Love each other as I have loved you.
- Forgive. And forgive again.
- Take my yoke on you and learn of me.
- Treat others as you would have them treat you.

Someone inevitably tells me these instructions are simply too difficult, so I ask the group to tell me what the first list, the "rules of engagement" of our culture, produce. Inevitably, there are quiet expressions and outbursts of frustration as words like stress, conflict, anger, ulcers, fear, resentment, divorce, and failure are spoken with such emotional impact that it seems those words are hanging in the air like balloons in a comic strip.

But nobody's laughing.

I follow up by asking about the results in the lives of people who take the "rules for the road" as their guiding principles, and the silence grows deeper. Finally, and almost wearily, people start responding.

"When I follow those rules, I have conflict everywhere I turn."

"Following the rules of the roads destroys my peace, and I don't like myself. I feel more like a machine than a human being!"

"I have no peace, and then I drink too much."

"I lose touch with my family. I lose touch with God. I lose touch with what matters most."

I allow time for the silence to deepen and for all of us to grasp the cost of enslaving ourselves to the unspoken rules of the our culture. Then, I ask what might be the results of following the Jesus way, and almost every time I have done this exercise in a group, the first word that is spoken is *peace.*

A stranger who had not said a word on a retreat I led and who had no idea that I was writing a book about keeping hope alive said, "You know, I've followed your 'rules of the road' for my whole life, and I am here to tell you that I have spiraled down into the darkest hole of hopelessness I have ever been in."

I have been seized by the power of a great affection.

—Brennan Manning, *The Ragamuffin Gospel: Good News for the Bedraggled, Beat-Up and Burnt Out*

He paused to control his emotions, and I swallowed the temptation to tell him that those are not my rules but the rules of a culture that values getting to the top and "being somebody" more than anything else. They are *our* rules, and we are injuring ourselves and each other as we wield them recklessly.

Gaining control of his emotions enough to talk, the man added, "I can see that if I could ever have the courage to do what Jesus taught, that might be the way of hope."

I believe that nurturing hope in each other is part of the mission of the church, and I believe that supporting each other in the attempt to at least try to follow Jesus' teachings is more necessary now than figuring out who stands on which side of the political or social issue *du jour.*

Here are some questions to consider: What difference does it make that we have just observed Easter as a community of faith if we do not integrate the resurrection into our daily lives? Is salvation about going to heaven when we die, or is there a difference in the way we live now if we claim to be a follower of Jesus? What does it mean, really, to "invite Jesus into your heart"? If you can't see yourself following the teachings of Jesus in your workplace or on the golf course, how do you feel about starting within this church or within your family?

I didn't plan on writing books about Jesus or teaching about Jesus.

In fact, some of the things about my Baptist past and Jesus bothered me when I was a preacher's kid, and some of the things about my Baptist present bother me, but the one thing that has grown in meaning and value in my history and in my current life is the belief in a personal, dynamic love relationship with the Living Christ.

I sing the old hymns about Jesus and trip over some of the simplistic or sentimental theology expressed in them, and I get edgy when we sing about heaven because I have come to the place of believing that whatever is on the other side of this life is up to God, and how we live now on this earthly plane is of vital importance. I'm committed to the definition of eternal life expressed by Jesus in John 17:3—eternal life is *knowing God.*

However I got to this place in my life—by my own choices or by fate or destiny—the pursuit of that mystery, the mystery of knowing God, has given my life meaning and purpose and, yes, radical hope.

He is risen! Christ is risen indeed!

The story of the resurrection of Jesus reveals the mystery and power and meaning of God's work in humankind.

Hundreds of times I have said that we who live in this century did not have the experience of seeing, touching, being healed by, and hearing the human Jesus that the people of the first century did, and yet, through remembering and observing the events of his life, through using our imaginations, and through the mysteries of prayer and meditation, we can "know" the Living and Resurrected Christ.

This year, the piece of the story of Jesus' crucifixion and resurrection that turned over and over in my mind was the cruelty of those who arrested him, beat him, and then put him on a criminal's cross. Man's inhumanity to man, inflicted on the personification of unconditional love—God-made-flesh—tormented me, and perhaps it was because the context of Easter season 2017 was filled with signs of violence all over our fragile planet in ways I have never imagined. That people continue to torture and kill other human beings two thousand years after Jesus' death, often in the name of their concept of a religious system, bothers me to my core.

For me the most radical demand of Christian faith lies in summoning the courage to say yes to the present risenness of Jesus Christ.

—Brennan Manning,
*Abba's Child: The Cry of the Heart
for Intimate Belonging*

The words that roll so glibly off the tongues of those within my religious world grate on my nerves.

"To think that Jesus would die on the cross for my sins."

"Jesus paid it all; we don't have to worry about our sins."

"Hate and fear are forever nailed to the cross!"

"When Jesus says, 'It is finished,' from the cross, we can be assured of his forgiveness of our sins!"

I tremble before the risk I am taking to question what others who have gone before me or those who speak from high places say, but I see the "finished" piece of the crucifixion more as a cry of completion from the tortured lips of Jesus, announcing that he had fulfilled his purpose in showing the world the nature of God.

I don't see the work of the cross meaning that I can live any way I please as long as I identify as a Christian. There is so much more to being a follower of Jesus, and that "burden" we are to take up as we follow him seems to be a life-time commitment of shedding one layer of unconsciousness, of brokenness, of sinfulness, of self-will after another and allowing the Living Christ and Holy Spirit to work in the depths of our lives to create healing, transformation, and redemption.

Let my trust be in Your mercy, not in myself. Let my hope be in Your love, not in health or strength, or ability or human resources.

—Thomas Merton

As I continued to ponder through Holy Week this year, it came to me that the crucifixion was the work of humans held in the clutches of legalism and greed and the need to control; the work of the resurrection, though, was the fullest expression of God's Spirit and unconditional love, mercy, and grace that announced to the world, "Love is greater than hate. Life is greater than death."

In the resurrection, God's power overcame the powers of control and greed.

In the resurrection, God's love overcame the powers of evil.

In the resurrection, God's love bequeathed hope into human beings, and his light overcame the darkness.

In the week after Easter 2017, a story was posted on the website for the Society of Saint John the Evangelist. Written by Brother Geoffrey Tristram and originally posted in April 2011, it captured my heart (http://www.newssje.org/2011/04/24/alleluia-br-geoffrey-tristram/).

In 1922 in Kiev, in the Soviet Union, revered Soviet politician Nikolai Bukharin spoke at an anti-religious rally, preaching atheism and casting scorn on those who believed in God.

At the end of the speech, the chairman of the events asked if there were questions. There was silence until an elderly man, dressed in the robes of an Orthodox monk, stood up in the back. Slowly, he made his way to the front of the crowd and climbed to the stage. Turning to the crowd, the old man raised his arms upward, and in a loud, confident voice, he cried out, "Alleluia! Christ is risen!" At once, the huge crowd rose and shouted out, "The Lord is risen indeed! Alleluia!"

Brother Geoffrey went on to say, "Resurrection was in the spiritual DNA of those people. However much they were told the opposite, however much they were forced to live as if there were no God, the seeds of hope lay deep in their souls, latent, waiting, watching—and those ancient words 'Christ is Risen' brought the seeds suddenly to life."

Brother Geoffrey added the lovely coincidence that the Russian word for Sunday—Voskresenive—is also the word for resurrection and that "the same seeds for hope are placed deep in our own hearts." Then he asked this question: "How do we allow those seeds of hope and resurrection deep within us to burst out into new life?"

Questions to Ponder

1. When it comes to Jesus, are you more curious, cautious, or committed?

2. How would you explain your answer to someone who is a committed follower of Christ?

3. How would you explain your answer to a skeptic?

4. When it comes to the teachings of Jesus, which ones do you find the hardest to follow? Which ones have changed your life?

5. If you accept that the human Jesus had to die in order for the risen Christ to be born, what does that mean for your life today?

6. What difference does being a Christian make in your life now, today?

Jesus makes me nervous, a stranger told me,
    but when I asked why, he shrugged
    and walked away.
    Maybe it's Christians who make him
    nervous.
I don't know about that Jesus person, a
    friend said, and I tried to maintain
    a neutral persona.
    I wondered what it was she didn't know,
    but I was afraid to ask.
Do you really still believe that Jesus story?
    a young sophisticate asked, or was
    he a weary old man at twenty-five?
    It was hard to tell because I
    couldn't discern whether he was
    a true cynic or a lost soul not
    wanting to be disappointed again.
Are you a follower of Jesus?
    If you are, why don't you tell me
    about him and how he's changed
    your life.
Eternal God, I want to be true to my words.
I want my life to reveal your love,
my words to match my ways.
    Make me wise if I am going to represent you.
    More, let your love flow through me,
    unhindered by fear.

Chapter 13

THE SECRET ROOM

While *practicing resurrection* is a choice to make, it is also an orientation toward life. It is a point of view that assumes that we human beings can experience life's challenges in life-giving ways. Grounded in an understanding that I don't always get my way about things but that God works to bring about wholeness, justice, and mercy in the most difficult circumstances, practicing resurrection is a choice to surrender my will to God. Often, that process involves dying to one's own will and way, a crucifixion of ego, in order to experience a resurrection.

What other spiritual practices can nurture the decision to practice resurrection? For me, a deep immersion in the life of Jesus, his teachings and his encounters with human beings during his earthly ministry, and a consistent practice of Centering Prayer are central to the spiritual path of practicing resurrection.

I have been moved to a deeper level of connection with holiness through music or in nature. I have felt touched by the holiness of God through the inspiration of the written word, and I have experienced sacred moments with family or friends or gathered with my community of faith. I have felt God's presence at the altar, receiving Communion, and I have sensed God's presence in solitude and silence.

In my life, the consistent practices of contemplative prayer and of immersing my mind and heart in the Scriptures through imagination have given me an inner experience of the presence of God, the companionship of the inner Christ, and the mystery of the Holy Spirit. These two practices, Centering Prayer and a conscious immersion in the Scripture, when *done intentionally* for the purpose of deepening my relationship with God, have changed my life.

Intention is everything. When I say my sacred word in Centering Prayer, that word expresses my consent to the presence and action of God within.

Intention expresses what I want to be true, even when I feel fear or anxiety, shame or guilt, insecurity or inadequacy, resentment or anger. My intention—to draw near to God and to allow him to draw near to me—says, "In spite of what I am feeling in this moment, I desire the presence and action of God within my circumstances."

When you pray, go into your room, close the door and pray to your Father, who is unseen. Then your Father, who sees what is done in secret, will reward you.

Matthew 6:6

Intention expresses my desire to surrender my stubborn will—my inordinate attachment to my ideas of how life or people should be—and moves me to the prayer of ultimate surrender: "Thy will be done."

Intention overrides my clinging to my will and expresses the deeper desire that I live and act and speak in harmony with the will of God.

Intention expresses my willingness to look straight into the face of disappointment and despair, failure and defeat, and be willing to allow the resurrection principle to work and to produce hope.

We cannot experience—see, hear, touch, be healed by—the human Jesus, but we do have access to the Living Christ, the Holy Spirit of Christ, through the practice of Centering Prayer and the immersion in the Gospel stories in prayer.

Fr. Keith Hosey first introduced me to the process of using imagination to put myself into the Gospel stories and of imagining that Jesus was with me. His teaching took the stories from the pages of the

Bible and from history and made them real, current, personal, and life-giving. Keith made the written word fresh to me and changed my approach to the Bible so that I could experience the Living Word for myself.

Over the past several months I have been teaching the miracles of Jesus as recorded in the four Gospels to two separate classes, my Thursday Morning Bible Study, composed of women from different religious backgrounds, and a Sunday morning co-ed Bible study class. Throughout these months, I have emphasized various principles that form the foundation of my teaching.

In the first place, we can read each of the miracles as an event in history and consider it a story that has nothing to do with us. We can even ask, "If I didn't live when Jesus lived and if I couldn't have access to his healing presence, what difference do these miracles make to me?" Further, we can believe that those miracles happened exactly as they are recorded, but what difference does it make if Jesus walked on water and calmed the storms in the first century if we do not allow the Living Christ to walk across the waters of our inner storms today?

Finally, after facilitating conversations with the people in my classes over these months, I realize that each miracle happened when an individual had a direct encounter with the human Jesus, and that fact holds a key to our lives today.

This all sounds good in theory, but how is a person supposed to relate to the story of Jesus, both the historical Jesus and the mystery of the Living Christ? How can you—a human being, grounded in the earth, relating to the outer world, bound by time and space in this realm—have a relationship with the resurrected Christ? How does the mystery of the resurrected Christ interface with the everyday, ordinary experience of going to work, running errands, and taking care of the mundane and routine obligations of daily life?

Again, practicing the presence of Christ, a well-used practice of contemplatives, and immersing myself into the stories of Jesus have made the Living Christ come alive for me.

I have seen people move from apathy about the miracles to curiosity about them, from indifference and even skepticism to a deepening faith in the reality of the presence and action of the Living

Christ. I have seen people move from doubt and even despair to faith by an immersion in these miracles. I have moved to what has been an amazing level of *hope* by opening my mind and imagination to the presence of the Living Christ, alive and active in my inner life, outside the control of my overactive ego-self.

I have often said that the only thing guaranteed to wake up fully refreshed and raring to go every single morning is my ego-self, the vehicle in which I get around in the world and the part of me that prefers and loves stability, predictability, familiarity, and the status quo. To move to an internal shift of being guided by the Christ within continues to be nothing short of revolutionary for me. It isn't easy, but practice really does make a difference.

It was early spring in West Texas, and the sky was a deep blue when I set out on my walk, taking a break from writing *Becoming Fire*, a book that offers seven days of readings that invite the reader to imagine being a character in one of thirty-three Gospel stories. These readings are, by the use of imagination, journaling, sitting in the silence with the story, and carrying the story with you over seven days, gateways to prayer and to experiencing the presence of the Living Christ.

For a couple of hours at my computer, I had immersed myself in one of the stories in the Gospels, imagining myself back in history, picturing myself as the various people in the stories of Jesus' human encounters—with the curious, the cautious, and the committed. I was energized from the writing process and the subject matter, and as I walked I was still in the zone of imagination but also fully connected to the street, the traffic, the sun and the slight breeze on my face.

The inner world is as real to me as the outer world.

The thought came unbidden, reflecting the reality of being able to access the inner kingdom about which Jesus spoke while staying grounded in the outer world. For the rest of that walk, I felt the joy of being connected to the outer world and the inner world and of letting my imagination work through my fingers and out onto the keyboard of a new computer.

The thought also startled me and fascinated me. As a people-pleaser, a codependent, a person who longs for approval and yearns to be free of the fear of disapproval, I was shocked at what had come into my mind. As a person who values relationships and whose priority has always been family and friends, I was being led from an inner source to a new understanding of myself.

I had no idea that what was ahead was a journey inward that would introduce me to the Christ within, the inner kingdom and my True Self. I had no way of knowing on that beautiful blue-sky day that I was beginning a long-term and sometimes tedious and always circuitous process of healing, transformation, liberation, and empowerment.

Sought through prayer and meditation to improve our conscious contact with God as we understand Him, praying only for the knowledge of His will for us and the power to carry that out.

—Step Eleven of the Twelve Steps

Now, years later, I know for sure that that process was initiated and guided by the Living Christ and that it would change my life forever. Even in that moment and without fully understanding what was happening in my interior world, I knew that entering into those stories in the Gospels with the power of the imagination was a life-altering process.

I have to smile at what came next to my mind.

If I could introduce the people in my world to the power of using the imagination to connect with the inner Christ, I will have fulfilled my purpose in life.

I smiled because it is so true to my nature as a teacher and writer to want to share what is life changing and thrilling, but I also know that we teachers often teach what we want to learn.

Some writing instructors say that you should write about what you know. There is truth to that guidance, but there is another side to the writing process. I have experienced the amazing reality that I write to *discover* what I must know!

Of course, I want to be a student of those excellent teachers who are well prepared and are experts in their fields. I do write and teach what I know, but what makes both adventures thrilling—and yes, sometimes daring and scary and startling—is knowing that setting out to teach a subject or write a book is to partner with the Source of creativity (God), who will take you into uncharted territory.

I now *hope* for that adventure because I know the learning curve is the way of growth.

I have learned that as long as we are growing not only intellectually but also spiritually, we are alive. Growing can produce anxiety, but I remember the words of Dr. Jim Hollis, author and current director of the Jung Center of Washington, DC: "If you can choose between anxiety and depression, always choose anxiety because anxiety is a sign you are choosing life."

You will keep in perfect peace him whose mind is steadfast, because he trusts in you.

Isaiah 26:3

Isn't it the oddest thing that daring and risking and being willing to try and fail are necessary to living a life of hope? Isn't it counterintuitive that learning to tolerate the discomforts of anxiety might be necessary to developing an internal wellspring of hope? I have learned that the resurrection principle is the growth principle, and that hope grows when I keep an open mind and heart to life, especially when it is complicated, confusing, and chaotic.

When confronted by what is different and uncomfortable, who among us doesn't react at times by backing off, shutting down, criticizing, or condemning? And do we express our fear by pushing back on what we don't understand and don't like?

Take a thorough look at the life of the human Jesus and you see a Jewish rabbi whose mission was to unsettle the status quo to reveal the nature of God and set people free. Read about the resistance Jesus experienced from the religious and political sectors and notice how true he stayed to his mission. He never allowed outer rebellion and

resistance to take him off his path and his purpose, from the tempta-
tions of the adversary in the wilderness to the agony of Gethsemane,
from the arrest and the betrayals and the trials to the torture and the
crucifixion.

The headline was written in the colors of the rainbow and made me
smile: *How to Dress Happy.* Below it was a short paragraph introducing various articles of clothing to raise the happiness quotient.
"They say that attitude is everything . . . . So, if you can't yet muster
the positive mind-set to take on the new year, fake it with your
wardrobe. With a whole new year ahead—and the worst of winter
upon us—we could all use a dose of sartorial Prozac" (*The New York
Times*, January 12, 2017).

There is nothing wrong with "dressing happy," and perhaps
there are days and seasons when dressing happy is an act of
kindness. The offerings in this article include rainbows on sweaters,
shoes, and jewelry; smiley faces on shirts; and other T-shirts that
convey messages to lift one's spirits and change the effects of winter's
gray skies.

My mother at age ninety said that she wore makeup as a public
service, and so perhaps we adults have an opportunity or maybe even
an obligation to convey an upbeat spirit, speak words of optimism,
and do things that show we can rise above winter's chills by wearing
happy clothes.

Actually, I can vote for that!

We have all experienced that person whose negative moods,
words, body language, or facial expressions can change the energy of
an entire room. We are powerful in shaping and affecting how other
people feel; emotions are seemingly contagious, and if we are not on
guard, we can catch each other's bad moods.

We can also put on a happy face to mask our true emotions,
essentially hiding the truth about our feelings below the surface. If
it's not appropriate to dump our bad mood or negative feelings on

others, can that falsely happy face be the right thing to do? It can be a kindness to restrain ourselves and deal with those afflictive emotions privately.

However, wearing such a mask can become your habitual way of being in the world. Though faked happiness can feel like escape to the person doing it, it looks like hypocrisy to those who can see below the surface. When done long enough, faking anything in the emotional world can reap a bitter harvest.

There is a problem if you don't take care of the inner turmoil or afflictive emotions. Polishing the outside of the cup, hoping to manufacture hope and hopefulness, is dangerous to you and unsettling to those who try to know the real person.

No spiritual practice is more valuable to my inner life than the ones I have learned from teachers of what is called the contemplative way.

From Brother Lawrence, who worked in a monastery kitchen in France in the seventeenth century, I learned the concept of *The Practice of the Presence of God*, which is also the title of a compilation of his wisdom about living in intimacy with God.

From Keith Hosey, who taught me the Ignatian way of entering into Scripture by using imagination, I learned how the Scriptures and the living presence of Christ can come alive in our lives.

From Andrew Murray, I learned the power of abiding in Christ by pouring over his classic *Abide in Christ*, and from Jesus' model, I learned the importance of drawing apart to a place of solitude for the purpose of listening to God, aligning with God and his will, and developing intimacy with God. From Jesus, too, I learned that the kingdom of God is within the human heart and soul.

From Sister Mary Dennison, my spiritual director at the Cenacle Retreat Center, I learned the way of *lectio divina*, a way of allowing Scripture to speak to your experience.

My teachers and spiritual directors all taught me necessary wisdom for living with a sense of connectedness to the presence of

God, and from them all I learned that "the One you seek also is seeking you." From these and others, I learned that the real security of the soul is in the knowledge that I live in the heart of Christ, who lives in my heart.

I learned the Jesus prayer from *The Way of the Pilgrim*, and now—a lifetime later—I know for sure that the teachings I sought and the ones that found me were absolutely necessary in developing my faith from my earliest acceptance of Christ into my heart to the practice of Centering Prayer, a practice that is the foundation of my prayer life.

I have learned to turn to the deepening of my Centering Prayer practice when the paths of life are overgrown with troubles from without and fears from within, and so it was natural to me to deepen that practice while facing one obstacle after another as I wrote this book. I believed that doing this faithfully would allow the Living Christ to nourish and nurture the grace of hope within my inner life.

One of Thomas Keating's most foundational teachings in the practice of Centering Prayer is the one about *the secret room.*

Of course, if you cut open a human body, you will not find that secret room or closet. No surgeon can find *the soul.* You will find a human heart—a pump, really—but the heart we talk about when we guide young children to invite Jesus into their hearts is something beyond that physical pump.

In the middle of winter I discovered within myself an invincible summer.

—Albert Camus

When we say that God's kingdom is within, what do we mean? This one thing I know: whenever I talk about the unconscious, the True Self, the soul, or the inner kingdom, people seem to know what I mean. The understanding of either may be elementary. It may be that people are uncomfortable talking about it, but I have not yet encountered anyone who doesn't understand that there is something other than our physical bodies and our conscious minds.

In Centering Prayer, we use what we call a prayer word or a sacred word to express the intent to allow the presence and the action of the

Divine Therapist in the inner kingdom, below the conscious mind, in the recesses beyond the ego and the places we do not yet know.

In the twenty minutes of the practice of Centering Prayer, we are simply making ourselves available to God. We trust that whatever God wants us to do at the innermost level of our being, we are willing to do it. The fruit of the Centering Prayer practice is manifested in daily life, but usually, the person who is practicing the prayer doesn't notice the fruit first.

In this unseen exchange, the abiding in Christ, God "talks to" our hearts more than to our minds. As Thomas Keating says, contemplative prayer is more like an embrace or a hug than it is a dialogue or intellectual exercise. The prayer word gives the Divine Physician, the Living Christ permission to pour love, joy, and peace into us without the ego's having to monitor or control the flow.

If you use the vine and branches metaphor in John 15, it can be said that the life of God flows into the life of the person in an open state of mind and heart much as the life force and nutrients flow naturally from the vine into the branches. Those nutrients then flow from the vine out into the gifts, the fruit, that are consistent with the particular vine!

> *The kingdom of God is within you.*
>
> Luke 17:21

The Divine Indwelling, as Keating also refers to the presence of God within us, can be unconscious to us, except perhaps as a longing for God. However, as we continue to practice Centering Prayer, we become attuned to that inner Voice, much as the sheep recognize the voice of their shepherd. The gift of that union with the Spirit of God are the three graces Paul writes about in 1 Corinthians 13 (faith, hope, and love), as well as the fruit of the Spirit he lists in Galatians 5 (love, joy, peace, gentleness, self-control, patience, goodness, generosity, and faithfulness).

I have often called the presence of God the inner GPS, guiding us to places we need to go, working in the midst of our circumstances to reveal his will to us, helping us know what to do and how to do it. God grants us direction from the inside of this inner kingdom out, granting us the gifts we need for the experience at hand. Through this intimate relationship with Christ, the uniqueness of the True Self is strengthened and manifested so that a person in alignment with the inner Christ doesn't look to the outer world for direction so much as he listens to the still, small voice within.

I believe God wants to work within our circumstances for good, and it is by aligning with his purpose, his love, and his nature that we become more attentive to where and how he is manifesting his will.

The practice of Centering Prayer helps me forgive what, on my own, I cannot forgive and tolerate what I thought I couldn't bear.

The practice of Centering Prayer is the wellspring of hope within me, and I place my hope in that Source and not an outer-world outcome and certainly not in another human being.

Centering Prayer connects me with an unending source of joy so that I can be in great sorrow and still not drown in my sorrows, but smile in the midst of them.

Smile in the midst of them? It might seem this means grieving people should be able to smile if they just pray the right way, but that isn't what I'm suggesting.

One of my favorite quotations and a foundation of my life is the wisdom of Teilhard de Chardin when he says that "Joy is the most infallible sign of the presence of God."

In John 15:10-11, Jesus expressed his desire that his joy might be complete in his disciples. In John 15, Jesus compares intimacy with the father to the intimacy of the vine and the branches, and he urges us to "abide in him" and to allow him to abide in us, implying a life-giving relationship. Dwelling in him or abiding in him are the same thing, he says in John 15:9, as living in a love relationship with him. And the result of that intimacy, Jesus states clearly, is joy that might be in us and made complete in us.

Through living with that idea over a lifetime, I have learned the difference between the joy that flows from intimacy with God (see John 17:11 and 13) and the happiness that is dependent on external factors. Thus, it is possible, and often heart-wrenchingly difficult, to experience sorrow and the presence of God/joy at the same time. This is not about smiling through your sorrows as a defense against pain and it is *not* about putting on a happy face. This is about experiencing the presence of God, even in times of sorrow. That presence gives us peace and joy.

This kind of joy is a gift of the Holy Spirit (see Gal 5:22–23) and cannot be forced or pretended, and in the practice of Centering Prayer, the awareness of the presence and action of the Living Christ/ Holy Spirit is cultivated, nurtured, supported, and strengthened, and without the effort of the ego, the fruit of that prayer is love, joy, and peace.

Practicing the Presence of God gives me the stamina I need to hold steady when the winds of change threaten to blow away all I have valued, and it helps me bear the burdens of others and my own burdens with a radical kind of hope that defies rational and logical thinking.

I'm the first to admit that the changes in the world today have thrown me off-balance from time to time. I have protested mightily and have declared that not all change is progress.

Nevertheless, as I continue this practice of prayer that allows God to pour his nature into me, I keep affirming the belief I hold dear from Romans 8:28: God is at work in all things, attempting to bring about good.

Jim Wallis, founder of Sojourners, says it this way: "Hope is believing in spite of the evidence, and watching the evidence change."

Of course, I question the times.

Will there be a nuclear war in my lifetime, in my children's and grandchildren's lifetimes?

Will my children be safe in this world of terrorists and superbugs?

Will democracy crumble? What will happen if America falls to tyranny?

Will we have enough money in retirement? Will we stay healthy?

What if it's true that Christianity in America is dying? What will happen to the church?

In the early morning, I turn out of blessed habit to the Source. I begin my sit, my Centering Prayer practice, by introducing my prayer word silently, expressing my consent for God to be with me, in me, for me, *present*. My prayer word also gives my consent for the Inner Christ, the Divine Therapist, to be *active*, and with that consent, I am giving the Holy One permission to go into the shadows and recesses of the places that are unknown to me, deep beyond my conscious mind, and do whatever he wants to do.

In other words, my prayer word is synonymous with "thy will be done," and I return to that prayer throughout the day, making small turnings to God at a signal light, a railroad track, a parking lot where I wait for a friend, my husband, a child.

The truth is, my consent for God's will to be done in me and in my life is a daring prayer, a radical affirmation of surrender of my will and my life to the will of God. It is a yielding to God, whose very name and character is Love. I surrender my will and my life to God with that prayer because I have learned that while God's ways may not be my ways, it turns out that the best place for me to be is in the center of his will, no matter what is going on outside of me or in the larger world.

In a message exchange with Deana Mattingly Blackburn, my life-long friend from college, she spoke a simple truth that leapt off my phone screen. "When people say *Oh, just have faith; God is in control,* I want to say that *God will not be mocked!* It's not that I don't trust God," she continued, "it's actually that I do trust him to be true to his character."

Those words from my friend, forged over a lifetime of her faithful pilgrimage, remind me that God's ways are not our ways and that turning my attention away from my idea of solutions toward the infinite mercy and wisdom of God settles my restless mind and heart. Life may be chaotic, it may be dismal and dark, and it may be awful at times, but God is always true to his nature, and his nature is unconditional love.

I have worked the Twelve Steps for most of my adult life for issues of codependency, and I have said before that the Eleventh Step holds it all together. Once I had gone through the first ten steps and came to the eleventh, I knew that if I wanted to maintain my serenity, have courage, and manifest wisdom, I was going to need to maintain a conscious contact with God.

Whether you call them abiding in Christ or practicing the presence of Christ, entering the secret room, the prayer of the heart, the prayer of silence, mediation, listening prayer, or seeking first the kingdom of God, the practices that nurture and support the mysterious union with Christ are vital to the maintenance of the inner wellspring of faith, hope, and love.

For me, that journey began with a child's prayer, inviting Jesus into my heart.

The journey continues as I am constantly learning just what it means for Jesus to live in my heart.

Making It Practical

1. Explore the teachings of Jesus. Look at the sayings where he gives a direct imperative, such as the ones below. Choose one of his injunctions and attempt to follow it as long as it takes for you to feel that you have integrated that teaching into your life.

- Love one another as I have loved you.
- Abide in me, and I will abide in you.
- Forgive seventy times seven.
- Love the Lord your God with all your heart, mind, and soul, and your neighbor as yourself.
- Seek first the kingdom of God.

2. Study people's encounters with Jesus that are recorded in the Gospels. Choose one of those people and encounters, and live with that story as long as it takes to see how you are like that person and how Jesus treated that person. Imagine you are that person and that Jesus is talking with you as he talked with him or her.

3. Choose one of the miracles Jesus performed and read about it every day for a week. What does that miracle teach you about the power of God in your life?

4. Take twenty minutes, once or twice a day, to sit quietly and imagine that Jesus is with you. Imagine that all you have to do is extend love to him.

5. Explore Centering Prayer. Learn about abiding in Christ or practicing the presence of Christ. (There are many books for exploring the teachings of Jesus. I offer my books, *Meeting Jesus Today: For the Cautious, the Curious, and the Committed; Becoming Fire;* and *Christ-Heart,* all published by Smyth & Helwys.)

How do I follow you, Jesus?
   How can I know you,
unseen as you are?
How am I supposed to
take your yoke upon my
shoulders and learn of you
in this present age?
   Expand my awareness,
Living Christ . . . . Lead me out into the
invisible world and into
my interior world and
show me how it is that I can
know you now love you now
         follow you.
   Ineffable Mystery,
Holy Other, Invisible Companion,
   help me see you
   help me hear the
whispers of your grace.
I believe, but more . . . I love you.
Draw me near to you . . . by my love
for you . . . and by your love for me
   into your presence, into your light.

Chapter 14

THE CALL TO PILGRIMAGE

One of the best decisions I have made in my life is to *practice resurrection.*

When I first read those words at the end of Wendell Berry's poem "Manifesto: The Mad Farmer Liberation Front," I knew that his directive in two words expressed my walking orders for the next phase of my journey. I had no idea precisely what Berry meant, and I had no idea what his words would mean for me, but I knew I had to embrace his directive and start walking forward with a new idea. I believed that if I answered the call to the journey, the path would unfold in front of me. I had just enough faith to take the first step.

In the way of pilgrimage, those two words beamed a light down my path. All I had done before had prepared me to take the direction in which the light was pointing.

Many times I have heard the call of the high country in Colorado, not knowing what I would see or experience but knowing that I wanted to follow the path to the peaks. I have willingly bounced and jostled up the winding mountain paths, up where the air gets thin, the temperature chillier, and the sun more brilliant. Signposts along the way with arrows pointing in one direction or another and signs warning of dangers ahead are helpful, but the truth is that I never quite know what I will see or experience at the mountaintop.

The trails are rough above the tree line as I move toward the top. I have no idea how long I can stay on the mountain; a storm can turn a sunny day cold and wet in a hurry, but the possibility of arriving at the peak of a mountain calls me to keep going forward. Finally, gazing down from a high vantage point is exhilarating, evoking wonder and gratitude.

Behold, I am making all things new.

Revelation 21:3

The first time I heard about labyrinths and the work of Lauren Artress, I knew I yearned to journey to Chartres Cathedral. I knew I had to be trained, but I had no idea how or when I would finally get to that grand cathedral.

The call to the labyrinth took me to San Francisco, and the yearning for a place I had never been persisted. Finally, thirteen years after that initial beckoning, I was on a train by myself, traveling from Paris to Chartres. From that time until this, the labyrinth has been a consistent part of my larger journey, but when I first began and took that initial step, I had no idea why I was called to do what I did or what I would find. I just knew the labyrinth was calling to me.

The journey of *practicing resurrection* reminds me of my pursuit of the mountain peak and the circuitous path of the labyrinth.

I will be forever grateful to Wendell Berry, for in these years that I have attempted to integrate the idea of practicing resurrection into my spiritual practice, I have come to understand more fully the power of one's approach to life.

I attempt to be a follower of Jesus, and so as I am not a life/death person but a life/death/Life person! If I believe in the resurrection, then the resurrection has something for me now, in this life, where I am!

By taking on the ways of practicing resurrection, I have understood the meaning of the crucifixion and resurrection more fully and have realized again and again how important it is to take what happened in Jesus' life and knead the story into my own experience. Indeed, in working with the accounts of the crucifixion and resurrection, I have come to understand more deeply the idea and reality of the Living Christ, and I expect to continue to wake to new understandings of this great mystery at the center of my faith.

Integrating the Jesus story into my life year after year, day by day, I have discovered surprising new capacities to persevere, to persist, and to be patient. I find myself willing to trust that the same Spirit who moved in the crucified Jesus to bring forth life will move in my failures and disappointments and bring about something new within me.

The biggest surprise for me has been that the decision to embrace the practice of resurrection has increased a sense of hope in God even as the practice has helped me let go of hope as wishful thinking or of hoping I get what I want.

Henry Blackaby, author of the popular *Experiencing God,* counsels people to look for where God is at work in a situation and then to align themselves with what God is doing. Practicing resurrection has opened my mind and heart to see where God is working more clearly and, having seen, to work on the side of hope, of new beginnings, of life and love.

Lewis Smedes's book *Keeping Hope Alive* has a subtitle: *For a Tomorrow We Cannot Control.*

Jungian analyst Pittman McGehee often comments that we live between a birth we didn't ask for and a death we cannot escape. Between birth and death, there is much we cannot control. As a lover of the work of Holocaust survivor Viktor Frankl, however, I affirm that my last great freedom is to choose how I will respond to what happens in my life, including how I respond to what I cannot control. It is part of my Twelve Step work, as well, to pray for and work for the serenity to accept the things I cannot change and the courage to change the things I can.

Living that Serenity Prayer has been a constant practice as I have learned to practice resurrection.

Many of the people I know spend inordinate amounts of energy shoring up the edges of their lives so that they can stay in control, gain control, or have some sense of power over their lives. The need to control and wield power over others or over external forces is often symptomatic of internal fears. Ironically, the more we humans try to control and the more we wield our power, the more likely we are to perpetuate the thing we fear the most: loss of control and power.

> *The willingness to consider possibility requires a tolerance of uncertainty.*
>
> —Rachel Naomi Ramen

Smedes's practical wisdom clearly addresses the reality that we don't always get what we hope for and want. Hoping long enough and fervently enough for what I want doesn't always bring me the results I desire. Sometimes inner hope has no room to flourish until I can let go of these desires.

No matter how much we pray, some people don't get well. Marriages fail. In spite of hope, dreams die and wars rage on. We are sometimes forced to give up what we treasure most. Good people suffer while it seems that those who do harm flourish, but in the midst of life's losses, endings, terrors, and troubles, the challenge of *practicing resurrection* has caused me to stop placing my hope in my desired outcomes and see hope as an inner resource and a gift from God. Instead of putting my hope in people, I understand now that ultimately, my hope is in God alone.

I can still wish for the things I want, and I can even say I hope for them to come true, but the bottom line is that hope is a gift from God, and God is the One in whom I am to place my hope.

With my choice to practice resurrection, I have new eyes to see evidences of hope all around me. My friend Charlotte Caffey sent me a text about her young grandson, who said while joining the family for prayers, "Jesus, you have the right to remain silent." This made me smile, but it also made me pray for the serenity, courage, and wisdom to allow the Holy One to remain silent! I pray for the ability to wait on God, to endure the waiting, and to trust God with my life.

My friend Teresia Taylor has struggled mightily in her fight with cancer, but in her suffering she has reached out to engage with other fellow sufferers in a way that staggers my imagination. Raw and honest about the brutalities of her disease, the spark of life and hope within her allows her to talk about being "fascinated with this mysterious journey home." Teresia Taylor's living hope has spurred me forward as I have written this book.

I watched as my friend David Livingston took a longtime friend with Alzheimer's to play golf every week for years, and I marveled at how his faithful friendship and thoughtful caring must have been a gift to both his friend and his friend's wife. This past year, what David kept doing became a sign of hope for me, a sign of the kindness and compassion that exist in all of us. In this situation, the act was not just an idea or a kind word but also a helpful gift over a long period.

When David's friend died, I expressed how much his faithful act of friendship had touched me, and I will never forget his response. "It was a great friendship," David said, "and helping him and his wife never felt like much of a sacrifice. It was natural. It was easy . . . and I got to play golf."

Wendell Berry's challenge, *practice resurrection*, spoken in his poem to a culture beset by constant change, chaos, loss, and gain, has changed my life, and I hope it is forever changed.

These verses from the Old Testament recorded in Habakkuk 3:17-19 express the power of *practicing resurrection*:

Though the fig tree does not bud and there are no grapes on the vines,
though the olive crop fails and the fields produce no food,
though there are no sheep in the pen and no cattle in the stalls,
yet I will rejoice in the LORD, I will be joyful in God my Savior.
The Sovereign LORD is my strength;
he makes my feet like the feet of a deer, he enables me to go to great heights.

My friend and iconographer Caroline Furlong painted an icon for me, a process that took well over a year. The carefully detailed and painted treasure depicts Mary Magdalene at the empty tomb of Jesus, who has chosen to appear first to her in the Garden of Gethsemane.

When Caroline asked me what I would most like to have her paint for me, I immediately chose this remarkable scene when the Risen Christ appeared to this woman who has for millennia been labeled a prostitute—though there is no evidence of that in any of the Gospels. In fact, in other gospels that are not in the biblical canon, she is known as "apostle to the apostles."

Whatever happened to Mary Magdalene in her encounters with Jesus so healed and transformed her that she must have instantly caught the wisdom, meaning, and spirit of his teachings. However she was changed, Jesus' appearance first to her after the resurrection is deeply meaningful to me.

On that morning at the garden tomb, Jesus identified himself to Mary and yet would not let her cling to him, which is evidence that he was in a new relationship with his ministry, with her, and with the disciples. Jesus empowered this woman and gave her a task, and so Mary Magdalene rushed to the disciples with the staggering news that she had seen Jesus.

Apparently, Jesus knew that Mary Magdalene's heart and mind were so open and receptive that she was the perfect one to see him in a new way. Perhaps her sense of the

> *If the Spirit of him who raised Jesus from the dead is living in you, he who raised Christ from the dead will also give life to your mortal bodies through his Spirit who lives in you.*
>
> Romans 8:11

mysteries of God was deep enough that she was able to recognize the Risen Christ. Clearly, Jesus trusted her with the message of his resurrection because she had proven herself trustworthy. Whatever the reason the Risen Christ revealed himself to this woman, Jesus transformed her with the message of his resurrection.

As I examine more closely Jesus' post-resurrection appearances to his beloved friends, I am struck by how he met each one at the point of his need, and in doing so, he entrusted his work to a band of imperfect human beings. It is that gift of his work and the entrusting of his mission to the disciples, even though they had run away in fear, betrayed him, and denied him, that strikes me as another example of the resurrection principle.

Being given another chance, and another, and even more after that is God's gift of the resurrection principle—a gift of mercy, grace, and a new start. Our response completes the loop of life; as we practice resurrection day by day, challenge by challenge, we are participating with God in redeeming the world, bringing healing, transformation, liberation, and empowerment to each other and out into the larger world.

I have no problem believing that the resurrection of Jesus happened, and I don't need to know how it happened. Nor does it trouble me how Jesus walked on water, turned water into wine, or healed the sick and raised the dead. I am comfortable with the incarnation of Christ, partly because I am comfortable with mystery. It is with my child's heart that I embrace each of those mysterious and miraculous events.

Furthermore, I continue to be fascinated by the idea that the human Jesus had to die in order for the Risen Christ to be born and for the spirit of the Living Christ to cascade down through the centuries and into my life, just as I can accept and wrestle with the death of my own ego to allow the True Self in me to emerge.

What amazes me and sends me to my knees in gratitude and awe is that God keeps on being patient with us and continues to persist in extending his unconditional love to us.

With more awareness than I can reasonably enjoy, I recognize there is a force within me that also betrays the Christ in me. As much as I hate to admit it, there is within me another force that sometimes acts up and makes me behave as Peter did when he turned coward and denied Jesus three times. I, too, sometimes consciously and sometimes unconsciously deny the presence of the Living Christ within my inner kingdom.

And yet I continue to practice resurrection. Practice is necessary because I keep experiencing new things and being invited into new challenges. I practice because I am not yet proficient, but I rest in the adage that practice makes perfect, even as I acknowledge that on this side of eternity, I'm always a beginner and perfection or whole-ness, while not achieved, remains a goal, a North Star that guides me forward.

In church and among church people, I learned from my parents that the people who make up any church are like people anywhere. All of us are flawed, imperfect, and selfish; we all want what we want and we all think we are right, until and unless we have been willing to face our shadow, admit our flaws and defects, and surrender to the power of God, the source of redemption and the only object worthy of our faith, hope, and trust.

Forget the former things; do not dwell on the past. See, I am doing a new thing! Now it springs up; do you not perceive it? I am making a way in the desert and streams in the wasteland.

Isaiah 43:18-19

I have learned about faith and hope and love from actual human beings within the various churches that have formed and nurtured my faith. In my parents, I saw radical hope, steady faith, and patient love lived out in daily life. I witnessed sorrow and suffering as well as the depths of God's comfort and love. I also saw how my parents dealt with people who hurt them and hurt the church.

The hope I was taught, mostly nonverbally, by people whose lives were living flames of radical, transformative hope in God.

"I put my hope and faith and trust in God and *do the next thing indicated*," my friend Catherine Darden says whenever we talk. Felled by a stroke, stripped of her freedom to work and drive after two brain surgeries, and forced to be dependent through a long, difficult, and frustrating recovery, Catherine showed me over and over how to live, trusting in God's provision and care.

I have observed my friend Charlotte Caffey caring for her grandchildren with stamina, strength, and patience that have astounded me. I have watched other friends as they have cared for their loved ones through difficulties that seem to have no end.

"My favorite hymn is 'It Is Well with My Soul,'" my reserved brother-in-law declared quietly in a Bible study class one Sunday, startling my sister. A Vietnam veteran, a survivor of terrible illnesses called by exposure to Agent Orange, and, finally, a victim of Alzheimer's, John Williams never had to shout his faith. His steady, quiet composure in the midst of war, his deep enjoyment of life and the world, his crooked smile and his ready laugh, his love for my sister and their son, and his calm acceptance of the ravages of disease are all inscribed in my heart. His loyalty to his values was unwavering, and his support of me in specific ways throughout my lifetime kept the embers of hope alive in my broken heart.

> *So, I say, live by the Spirit. . . . Since we live by the Spirit, let us keep in step with the Spirit.*
>
> Galatians 5:16, 25

"There is every reason to be hopeful!" my spiritual director told me in the middle of a dark night of the soul. I believed her and allowed her to guide me to a new level of hope, and the hope within her ignited hope in me.

All my life, I have been around people who have been living witnesses to me of the resurrection principle. That spark of life, that inner wellspring, that amazing grace of hope provides stamina, strength, resilience, and persistence and radiates to others, striking a spark of hope and courage in those they encounter. It fills the empty cups of others with their overflow of hope.

I have been privileged to know people who live in service to their gift or calling, serving their talents with faithfulness. Aware of the responsibility of serving their gifts, they have submitted to passionate discipline, endured setbacks and disappointments and even failures, only to be stronger and more effective because they have learned from their mistakes. Instead of being arrogant about their unusual giftedness, there is a sense of astonishment and humility toward the gift, as if to say, "This comes from me?" or "You want me to do this?"

We humans still crucify the spirit of Christ over and over when hate triumphs over love, guilt and shame beat out mercy, fear destroys courage, despair obliterates hope, and legalism wins over grace. And yet the resurrection of Jesus stands as the triumph over death, over evil, and being committed to that life-giving energy is the call to the high road.

I have set before you today life and death, blessing and curse. Therefore, choose life.

Deuteronomy 30:19

The incarnation of Jesus, the miracles he performed, the resurrection, and the ascension all intrigue me, but I can be at peace with mysteries I neither explain nor fully understand.

The faithful people in my life have shown me the *resurrection principle* and what some call *resurrection power*. Like Mary Magdalene rushing to tell the disciples about having seen the Risen Christ, I feel an urgency to tell the people around me about the power of hope that is born from the heart of God. It is the life-changing, life-giving, transforming, healing, liberating, and empowering God-energy that lies in the heart of every believer. However faint that spark of hope and power is, it can be fanned into flame by the God whose very life is in all of us.

> The resurrection does not solve our problems about dying and death. It is not the happy ending to our life's struggle nor is it the big surprise that God has kept in store for us. No, the resurrection is the expression of God's faithfulness . . . . The resurrection is God's way of revealing to us that nothing that belongs to God will ever go to waste. What belongs to God will never get lost. (Henry Nouwen, *Our Greatest Gift*)

The words of Br. James Koester from the Society of Saint John the
Evangelist that leapt from my computer screen on a pre-dawn Lenten
morning blessed me then and bless me now.

> I believe that the good news of the passion, cross, and death of
> Christ is that he suffered most not because he was tortured, but
> because he loved much. It was because of love that he suffered.
> It was because of love that he died. And it was because of love
> that he rose again. As Dame Julian of Norwich says, "love was the
> meaning" not only of Christ's birth, but also his death.

On a warm June day, I headed to Galveston for solitude and silence
and the time and space to prepare to write my next book. A friend
had suggested that I might be interested in some jewelry that was
being made from the stained glass windows of Trinity Church, and
so, on a whim, I stopped by the church. Frankly, I dropped in to
see the jewelry only because my friend had suggested it. I had more
important matters on my mind.

Trinity Episcopal Church in Galveston sits within walking
distance of the seawall, a proximity that made it especially vulnerable
to the ravages of Hurricane Ike.

On that warm summer day, it was my good fortune to meet the
person who gives the tours of the church. Trish Clason had worshiped
within that community of faith for her entire life, and her children
are fifth-generation members of the church. Trish told me calmly
that she had lost everything in Hurricane Ike in September 2008.

As we walked around the church, I learned about the history
about Trinity Episcopal Church, dating back to its founding in 1841.
I heard about the beginnings of the church, and I heard how Ike had
ravaged it.

I heard about the faith of the people of that church, lived out in hard work, sacrifice, and the refusal to give up. Trish showed me how high the water had been and told me how water and sludge and utter filth mixed with chemical from the refineries, dead things, and mud. She described the stench and the devastation that had filled their sacred space.

She told me that after Hurricane Ike had devastated Galveston and damaged their building, the church had worshiped together every Sunday for two and a half years without air conditioning or heat—and had not missed a Sunday. "Now," she said, "God has sent us a new priest, and we are so happy."

At one point, I stopped her narrative and said, "You really love this church, don't you?" She beamed at me and said, "I do. I love this church."

We finally stopped at the altar. It felt as if we were standing on holy ground.

Over the altar of that historic church is a magnificent stained glass window made by the famous Louis Comfort Tiffany of New York in 1904. The window is a depiction of Jesus, with little children gathered all around him. The window shows the intention of the church, to minister to the littlest and the least.

For you were once darkness, but now you are light in the Lord. Live as children of light . . . .

Ephesians 5:8

The window is stunning, especially when the late afternoon sun beams through the image of Jesus. My guide told me about how the window had withstood countless other storms, but Ike in its fury knocked out a section at the bottom of that treasured Tiffany window.

Quietly, my guide shared with me how a former rector's wife had appeared at the church after the storm and, on her knees, had sifted and sorted through the mess and muck, gathering the shards of the stained glass from that window, carrying them home in buckets.

The woman carefully washed the shards, and then, in the amazing ways of life-affirming creativity, she was inspired to take the mess of broken and shattered glass to a jewelry designer and to people who could transform the glass into beautiful hand-crafted jewelry. In the words of the sponsors of this Phoenix Project, these pieces of jewelry are symbols of faith's ability to bring new life and new hope from disaster. Indeed, this jewelry project represents the rising from the watery ashes of a killer storm.

This is a story that has deep personal and symbolic meaning for me.

Life sometimes blows furious storms into our lives, storms that forever change the configurations of our families or our lifestyles. Sometimes we are rocked to the core by an event, a crisis, a natural disaster, or a betrayal, and from that time on, we look back and say, "On that day, everything changed."

I have come that you might have life, and life in its abundance.

John 10:10

Few people escape those terrible moments when, at the beginning of the day, you have one idea of who you are and how your life is going, and by the next day, you know that nothing in your life will ever feel or be the same.

I left my tour of Trinity Episcopal Church with a new necklace, a silver cross with shards of the Tiffany window, and with a new image of what it means to live with hope and faith and trust. Driving along the seawall, I was filled with awe and respect for people who are willing to get on their hands and knees in the terrible messes of life and get their hands and clothes dirty in order to salvage the shards of what is precious.

Parking at the seawall, I carried my folding chair as close to the water as possible. For the next hour or so, I breathed in and out deeply as I absorbed the sounds of the waves coming in and going out. With each wave, I breathed out whatever was blocking my sense of God's mercy and grace and breathed his hope into my heart, mind, and soul.

With every breath, I breathed out pain and sorrow and breathed in healing.

With every wave that came in and then went out, I felt increasingly connected to the energies of God's love, to the mysteries of life, and to the people whose acts of faith, hope, and trust have sustained them and me.

There in the cathedral built of sand and sun and sea, I gave thanks for the people of Trinity Episcopal Church.

Suddenly, a revelation made me catch my breath: what they are doing, I thought to myself, is *practicing resurrection*—and I wept.

After making practicing resurrection a conscious spiritual practice, I know that life is stronger than death. Love is stronger than hate. Hope is stronger than despair. And choosing life gives God consent to water the seeds of hope and beam the warmth of his power into our darkness.

God's part is to work in the details of our lives, some of which are invisible to us.

Our part is to practice the ways of faith and hope and life.

Therefore, practice resurrection. Practice it every day.

Questions to Ponder

1. When it comes to your spiritual path, what are the best decisions you have made?

2. Where have you seen God at work and chosen to join him?

3. What's next on your journey? Where might hope take you?

4. For whom are you a light, showing someone the path of life, of hope, of resurrection?

You've turned my life around
and made me see with new eyes.
　　You've opened my heart
　　and You have shown me love.
Certainly, You've stretched my mind,
　　challenged my preconceptions,
and shown me how pettiness,
prejudice, and intolerance
close my mind and shut down my heart.
　　Living Christ, You have
changed me in ways I didn't know
I needed to be changed.
　　In your grace, You wouldn't
leave me like I was, even when I
resisted.
　　May I remember that
it was You who put
me on this bumpy, winding
road to resurrection.
　　Give me the courage to
to keep on saying Yes to You.
　　Day by day,
　　I put my hope in You.

Made in the USA
Lexington, KY
26 January 2018